D0742548

Studies in Child Development

The Challenge of Thalidomide

WITHDRAWN
UTSA LIBRARIES

Studies in Child Development

WITHDRAWN
UTSA LIBRARIES

The National Bureau for Co-operation in Child Care

The Challenge of Thalidomide

A pilot study of the educational needs of children
in Scotland affected by the drug

by M. L. KELLMER PRINGLE
and D. O. FIDDES

R X T S A

LIBRARY
The University of Texas
At San Antonio

WITHDRAWN
UTSA LIBRARIES

LONGMAN
in association with
THE NATIONAL BUREAU FOR CO-OPERATION IN CHILD CARE

LONGMAN GROUP LIMITED
London
Associated companies, branches and representatives throughout the world

THE NATIONAL BUREAU FOR CO-OPERATION IN CHILD CARE
Adam House, 1 Fitzroy Square, London W1

© *The National Bureau for Co-operation in Child Care 1970*
All rights reserved. No part of this publication may
be reproduced, stored in a retrieval system or
transmitted in any form or by any means – electronic,
mechanical, photocopying, recording or otherwise –
without the prior permission of the copyright owner.

First published 1970

ISBN 0 582 32448 3

Printed in Great Britain by Spottiswoode, Ballantyne and Co Ltd
London and Colchester

LIBRARY
The University of Texas
At San Antonio

Contents

Foreword

Handicaps have two faces. One face, looking inwards, can be called absolute, the other face, looking outwards, relative. The obvious effects of thalidomide on the developing fetus are certainly seen in a plethora of absolute handicaps on and in the bodies of the affected children. The relative effects remain to be revealed by life. The measure will be the extent to which the absolute handicap is allowed to injure personality, to jeopardise social adjustment and to cramp intelligence.

Much has been learned about what emotional deprivation can do to slow down intellectual growth, some of it through the work of Dr Kellmer Pringle herself. No-one now disputes the need felt by every child to be loved and valued, to feel secure and confident, and to be given the chance to love in return. Deny the child this birthright and intelligence suffers. Physical handicap can easily disturb and prevent the fulfillment of these needs, first through the stress placed upon the family itself and second through a faulty school environment. For the children with congenital limb defects rocks and reefs lie ahead in the stormy seas of adolescence, but they should now be secure in harbour being educated and prepared for life.

It is on this period when education is the priority that Lady Hoare and the Fund for Thalidomide Children wish to focus attention. What can be learned of the intellectual potential of these affected children? How are they being handled within the educational system? How much absolute handicap is still compatible with normal schooling? How sensible or how necessary is placement of a given child in a physically handicapped school? What improvements could be suggested while there is yet time? The account which Dr Kellmer Pringle and Mrs D. O. Fiddes present in this report can provide a safe base from which these questions can be answered. And as with everything connected with

handicapped children, thalidomide with a dramatic intensity highlights their problems and forces them on the attention of all.

ALFRED WHITE FRANKLIN,

M.B., B.ch., F.R.C.P.

Immediate-past President British Paediatric Association,
Physician-in-Charge, Department of Child Health,
St Bartholomew's Hospital

Acknowledgements

Many more individuals and organisations than can be listed here have given help with this project, but some must be singled out for special mention. The Lady Hoare Thalidomide Appeal not only initiated and financially supported the enquiry, but throughout gave all possible assistance to further its progress; the Physician Superintendents of the Royal Edinburgh Hospital and Gogarburn Hospital, Edinburgh, agreed to release Mrs D. Fiddes for a session each week for six months; Edinburgh University generously provided premises in the Godfrey Thomson Unit for Educational Research and Dr A. E. G. Pilliner, the Director of the Unit, kindly proffered hospitality and showed unfailing interest.

Mrs Barbara Muir acted as Secretary to the project; her assistant and all other members of the Unit staff gave valuable help in various ways whilst the project was housed with them.

Special mention should also be made of the following: the Directors of Education of the Local Authorities and their staff, particularly in Aberdeen City, Inverness, Banff and Edinburgh who were asked for, and readily provided, additional facilities; the head teachers and class teachers of all the individual children who willingly supplied information; Mrs I. C. Douglas, the Lady Hoare Thalidomide Fund's Social Welfare Officer in Scotland; Dr D. C. Simpson, Director of the Bio-Engineering Unit, and Miss Hunter (House Mother of the Thalidomide Self-Care Unit) at the Princess Margaret Rose Hospital, Edinburgh; the Women's Royal Voluntary Service, its local organisers, and the members who provided transport and escort services; the British Red Cross, Scottish Branch, who offered similar help; and above all, the parents, relatives and guardians of the children and, last but not least important, the children themselves.

To all these and many more our warmest thanks are offered for help, co-operation and encouragement given in all kinds of ways to the many aspects of the survey.

Valuable suggestions were made by five readers of the final manuscript: Mr R. Gulliford; Dr Ann Mullins; Dr Jessie Parfit; Dr Mary Wilson and Dr A. White Franklin. Invaluable help with the editing was given by Mr W. L. Hooper, the husband of one of us (M. L. K. P.). While we are most grateful for the resulting improvements, the shortcomings of this book are entirely our responsibility.

M. L. K. P. and D. O. F.

1. Educating the Handicapped Child

When attention is focused on a hitherto neglected handicap, such as autism, or when a new handicap emerges, such as thalidomide, there is a renewed risk that needs and remedies will be considered in isolation– as if they were basically different from what is required for other handicapped children; just as there is a tendency to overlook the fact that the basic needs of the disabled child are the same as those of his non-handicapped brother. To set this study of thalidomide children within the necessary wider framework, it is preceded by a brief consideration of the various issues which arise in educating any and every handicapped child.

1. Learning and emotion

Implicit in much educational thought is the assumption that emotion and learning are separate and distinct from each other. In fact, intellect and feelings so constantly interact and modify one another that they are almost indivisible. The presence of a disability poses special problems but the basic emotional and educational needs are shared by *all* children. Many would argue that not enough attention is paid to them in the upbringing and education of children generally and that the consequences of this are reflected in the incidence of emotional maladjustment and educational difficulties. For the child who has a disability to start with, the consequences are likely to be more serious still.

What then are these basic needs? For most practical purposes a fourfold classification is sufficient, namely the need for love and security, for new experiences, for recognition and achievement, and for responsibility.

The first need is perhaps the most important during the long and difficult business of growing up. It is unconditional acceptance which gives the child this sense of security, the sense of being cherished whatever he may be like and whatever he may do. This is the basic and all-pervasive feature of parental love – valuing the child for his own sake.

What are the special problems faced by the handicapped in relation to this need? To give a sense of security, one needs to feel secure oneself. But this is just what many parents of a handicapped child do not feel: some are overwhelmed by their lack of knowledge and afraid that they may not be able to meet his special needs; others feel guilty or ashamed; others may be completely at a loss, especially parents of slow-learning children who themselves are of limited ability and thus too bewildered by all the other demands of modern life to give adequate emotional support to their handicapped child. In the great majority of cases not enough is done to help them to face and come to terms with their own unconscious attitudes and fears (Tizard and Grad, 1961). At school, too, special difficulties are likely to arise unless the child is among the lucky few for whom an early and correct diagnosis is made, a place is available in a suitable school, whether ordinary or special, and long-term educational guidance, in the fullest sense of the term, is provided throughout his school life.

It is entirely natural that parents feel concerned, and often anxious. Indeed, these feelings could be harnessed to provide the motivation for giving that extra care, time and thought to the handicapped child which are so essential in helping him to overcome as far as possible, the adverse effects of a disability. Instead, this natural concern often turns into over-anxiety or resentment: left without a full understanding of the nature of the handicap or of its short-term as well as its long-term implications, parental uncertainty may show itself in insecure and inconsistent handling. The more severe, complex or multiple the handicap, the more urgent the need for comprehensive diagnosis and continuous guidance.

The second basic emotional need is for new experiences. For the small baby everything that goes on around him falls into this category; so does every one of his earliest achievements, be it the ability to move his limbs or to examine the texture, taste and appearance of materials and objects, while learning to understand speech and to talk himself makes possible a vast range of new experiences. New experiences can, in fact, be regarded as a prerequisite for growth. A child's ability to learn, to respond to education in the widest sense of the word, depends not only on his inborn potentiality or intelligence, but equally on the stimulation and opportunity for new experiences provided by his environment.

How does the handicapped child fare regarding the satisfaction of this need? Inevitably the nature of the handicap will distort, delay or even make impossible the acquisition of at least some new experiences. Little is known as yet about how each handicap distorts learning; for example, the physically handicapped may fail to acquire experience of space and movement which may distort concepts of distance, dimension and later of number; the deaf, because of their difficulty in acquiring language until much later and to a more limited extent than normal children, may fail to acquire an adequate basis for abstract thought. Not only is it inevitable that early learning is delayed or distorted, but this is a cumulative and progressive process. The way in which this affects the quality of learning awaits detailed exploration. Meanwhile the ingenuity of parents and teachers will be taxed to the full if they try to provide and adapt new experiences to the child's limitations without curtailing the range of those experiences more than is absolutely necessary.

Modifications may be needed in the order and manner in which new experiences are presented; more careful grading and control may have to be used and the aid of specially devised tools, gadgets and apparatus may have to be called on to minimise difficulties and failure. Otherwise there is a danger that new experiences may become a source of anxiety and defeat instead of an exciting challenge. One effective way of learning, open to all handicapped children, except the deaf, is through speech. For some, such as the physically severely disabled, it can become a compensatory way of broadening their experience and understanding. This means that talking to him and encouraging him to speak from the earliest age is even more important for the handicapped than the normal child. In this way he learns to think about his experiences and his environment.

The third need, for recognition and achievement, is closely linked with the previous one. Just because learning is a slow and arduous process, even for the normal child, a strong incentive is needed. This lies in the pleasure shown at success and in the praise given to achievement by the adults whom the child loves and wants to please. Encouragement and a reasonable level of expectation act as a spur; too little expectation leads the child to accept too low a standard of effort; too high expectations make him feel that he cannot live up to what is required of him which leads to discouragement and diminished effort. An optimum level is geared to each child's capability at a given point in time and at a given stage of growth – a level where success is possible but not without real effort.

In relation to the handicapped child there are twin difficulties here, made more intractable because they are based on assumptions which are rarely made explicit and of which we are barely conscious. The first is that we habitually praise for achievement rather than for effort. This is unjust at best and positively harmful at worst; for example, a physically handicapped child may have written only a few lines of composition but it will have cost him a great deal more in terms of concentration and effort than the normal child needed to produce twice as much; yet he is much more likely to be commended for his work. Linked to this is the general tendency to judge the success of the handicapped by the extent to which their achievements equal those of the normal majority. In consequence, the more severe the handicap, the less likely will the child be rewarded genuinely and unreservedly by recognition and a sense of real achievement.

Thus if this need is to be met, the handicapped must be granted the fulfillment of another need, aptly described by Mallinson (1956) as 'the need to be different and the need to be the same'. To do so it is necessary not only to recognise that the basic needs are shared by all children, but also to make all necessary allowances for the differences imposed upon the handicapped child by the nature of his disability. From this it follows that each child should be encouraged to compete only with himself, since if each one is individual, the handicapped child is even more unique. This means that even the slightest improvement over his previous performance is worthy of praise and recognition: the physically handicapped child who manages to walk a few steps unaided; the deaf child who repeats, though imperfectly, a word previously quite beyond him. The effort involved in making these small steps forward is colossal compared with the progress made by the normal child with relative ease.

The fourth need, for responsibility, is met by allowing the child to gain personal independence; first through learning to look after himself in feeding, dressing and washing himself; later in permitting him increasing freedom of movement without supervision about the home, street and neighbourhood as well as increasing responsibility for his own possessions and finally by encouraging him to become entirely self-supporting until eventually he may assume responsibility for others, at work or within his own family.

Inevitably the nature of a child's handicap may set a limit to the ultimate degree of responsibility he will become capable of exercising. But there is a tendency to set too low a limit from a sense of pity or over-protection, or else through underestimating what he might become able to do. There is a need to guard against a whole household revolving around the handicapped child; rather he should be given the opportunity both at home and in school, to shoulder some responsibilities, however limited in scope. In this way, self-respect and self-acceptance are fostered. How a child feels about himself and his handicap is a much more potent factor in determining his personal and social adjustment than the nature or even the degree of his disability.

2. Educating and supporting the family

Every parent wants to have a normal child and most mothers fear they may give birth to a deformed one. When this fear becomes a reality, a sense of guilt, feelings of rejection and a determination to make up, almost to atone, to the child for what has happened to him, are likely to be present to various degrees. Fortunately, rejection usually becomes modified; in some cases, however, it may turn into over-protectiveness and over-possessiveness which eventually can become as damaging as the handicap itself. There is no easy way of helping parents to face and manage these problems, no golden rule and no short cut. However, there is no doubt that the sooner the child's handicap and all its implications are considered as openly but also as supportively as possible, the better for all concerned. As Kershaw (1961) succinctly puts it: 'The temptation to procrastinate may be considerable . . . it is not always necessary to tell the whole truth at once with uncurbed frankness. A spade is a spade; there is no need to call it a 'bloody shovel' but it is dishonest and useless to pretend that it is a silver spoon.'

Early, comprehensive, multiprofessional and continuous assessment is essential for every child; both deficits and assets need to be considered so that the latter can be developed and the former minimised; both short-term and more tentative long-term plans need to be made; and from the outset the parents must be accepted as partners, both in the diagnostic and treatment procedures, be these medical or educational. At the same time, they will need expert advice about available resources within the community and in the more specifically educational field. Regular counselling services, both on an individual and a group basis, should be readily available to them, particularly at crucial stages in the child's life – shortly after his birth; during the vital early years; when he starts school and then at transition periods, from primary to secondary, from day to residential, from ordinary to special school; and during adolescence when new problems are likely to arise in relation to sexual maturation, vocational training, occupational choice and eventual emancipation from parental control.

3. Schooling for the handicapped child

Because trained intelligence can make up or at least compensate for physical and sensory disabilities it is essential to consider the child's educational potential and needs early and to plan well ahead. To begin with, every handicapped child should at least once be looked at as a growing individual whose special problems deserve special attention 'in the round'. This means a physical, psychological and social investigation so that all the factors, which have a bearing on deciding the most suitable educational placement, can be taken into consideration.

Hitherto generally accepted ideas – many of which were incorporated in the 1944 Education Act – are now being questioned: is a special school the best place for most handicapped children or should it be the last resort, as tends to be the case in the U.S.A.? What are the advantages of special classes attached to ordinary schools as against day special and residential schools respectively? Is the 'comprehensive' special school more in tune with current conditions – both in relation to educational theory and in the light of newly emerging patterns of handicap? What is the optimal balance between a child's emotional and educational needs and how can this best be achieved? Clearly, most of these issues cut across specific handicaps and it is highly unlikely that meaningful generalisations can be made in relation to any one handicap, least of all thalidomide which does not result in an exclusive or specific type of defect.

The starting point for current thinking can be summed up by saying that the ideal is for a handicapped child to live at home with his own family and to attend an ordinary day school. Now this may sound obvious (to the point of being simple minded or not worth saying), but this has not always been so. For example, blind babies were thought to require special training from the earliest moment and so were taken from their homes into the residential setting of Sunshine Homes during the preschool years. The present climate of opinion favours parental and community care. From this it follows that removing a child from his home is considered advisable only if remaining with his family is likely to hinder or even harm his physical, emotional or intellectual development; and that attendance at a special school is advisable only when the ordinary school cannot provide the special methods or equipment which are needed to ensure the child's physical, emotional and educational progress.

Practice is, of course, far less straightforward, clearcut and tidy. Home and community care can only work if the community cares in the sense of providing the necessary supportive and ancilliary services; these range from adaptations of houses and classrooms to home helps, counselling, part-time specialist teachers and special day schools within manageable travelling distance. And some ideas, such as a comprehensive school for the various types of handicap, have hardly been tried out in this country except for the severely, multiply-handicapped child and except in Scotland.

Basic to any planning is the premise that handicap is not a static condition, but as much a developing process as growth itself. Hence, planning too must be dynamic rather than static; assessment cannot be adequately done by a 'one man team', however eminent the specialist, but requires a basic team consisting of a doctor, a psychologist and a social worker. The most comprehensive assessment and the most adequate long-term planning are of little avail unless they are matched by equally adequate (both in quality and quantity) treatment facilities, be these medical, educational or social.

Adequate educational facilities mean to begin with, schooling which fosters emotional and social development as well as the acquisition of specific skills and knowledge; this can be supplemented, where required, by remedial and therapeutic measures, be these for general or specific learning difficulties, such as reading retardation, speech defects or impaired hearing. Where these difficulties are severe, intensive and prolonged, help may need to be given in a clinic or special school but milder forms can be catered for and overcome within the ordinary school.

Then vocational preparation needs to be thought of much earlier than at present and certainly earlier than for the normal child. This does not mean vocational training or education in the narrow sense of focusing on a particular kind of job. Rather it means making some forecasts, largely of a negative kind, to rule out certain types of employment, based on how much useful sight, hearing or speech there is, the range of skilled movement in arms and hands, the ability to walk or stand for substantial periods and the like. In this way, certain jobs may be ruled out fairly early – say at the beginning of the secondary stage of schooling – while leaving open at this time as many options as possible. When the child's general education widens out into science, language and practical subjects, skilled and experienced teachers may be able to observe the flowering of hitherto unsuspected potential as well as any new limitations imposed by the handicap on the acquisition of more complex achievements.

Not until the last two years in school need specific vocational preparation be considered. Indeed, even this suggestion is controversial. It can be argued that since the handicap, as well as the need for treatment, is likely to have interfered with educational progress, a prolonged rather than a curtailed period of general education is required. Starting vocational preparation and training prematurely might debar a youngster from, say, acceptance for a technical training course because of an inadequate basic grounding in mathematics.

In any case, unless a secondary school is large, it cannot readily provide a wide enough range of vocational opportunities. In some areas informal links with industry make it possible for extended periods to be spent on a part-time basis in a variety of workshops and offices; in others, special assessment centres have a part to play in aiding the handicapped school leaver in his vocational choice. The youth employment service has a key role in this forward planning and in building a bridge from the pupil-centred educational environment to the world of open or sheltered employment via assessment procedures and training courses. Even for the normal young person these transition stages can be beset by difficulties; for the handicapped they are almost bound to be times of anxiety, uncertainty and hence additional strain.

Since the two most frequent disabilities found among our group of thalidomide children were physical handicaps and hearing impairment, their educational implications should be singled out for special comment. In many cases, the education of the physically disabled child gets interrupted by the need for surgical interventions or other treatments either continuously or at intervals stretching over a number of years. Both in the initial assessment and in the long-term planning, the role of the orthopaedic surgeon is crucial. Though no specialist likes making long range forecasts, it helps teachers and parents to know both the most favourable and least favourable prospects, depending on how successful treatment turns out to be. This forecast should be in functional terms: for example, whether eventually the child will be able to stand and walk, with or without the aid of crutches, calipers or an artificial limb; or whether he will remain dependent on a wheelchair. If treatment is needed or a series of operations, it helps to know in advance their timing, how long hospitalisation will have to last on each occasion and whether this has to be followed by a period of physiotherapy, and so on. Though for obvious reasons, only rough indications can be given, forward planning should take into account the child's educational needs; for example, prolonged interruption of schooling is more critical at certain times than at others, or conversely, given advance notice, some adjustments can be made in educational procedures. If, on the other hand, the child's disability is likely to be permanent and will not require any major surgery or treatment, it is also helpful that everyone concerned should be aware of this.

Whether a physically disabled child is better placed in an ordinary or a special school depends not only on the nature and degree of the impairment, but on his personality, home background and parental attitudes. A detailed knowledge of the two types of school in question also has an important bearing on this most difficult issue: will this particular child make a better social and emotional adjustment, and hence probably better educational progress, if he is placed with normal or with other handicapped children? There can be no certainty – only probability. The special school has both advantages and disadvantages:

classes are smaller and hence more individual attention can be given; if it is a good school, then all the work will be based on small groups rather than class teaching; on the other hand, each class is likely to contain a very wide ability range, from the educationally subnormal to potential G.C.E. candidates, so that the pace may not be challenging enough for a really bright child and not slow enough for the educationally subnormal. For those not severely disabled, a start in an ordinary school may be worth a trial and conversely, a pupil who is doing well during his early years in a special school, should be considered for transfer to an ordinary one if he appears to need an educationally more challenging environment. However, decisions can only be taken in the light of all the evidence and at every stage there needs to be flexibility to take into account changes both in the child's development and in his environment.

The educational problems of the hearing impaired child are even more complex. 'The tragedy of deafness lies not merely in the handicap itself, but in the relationship of those who can hear to those who cannot. All other handicapped people, whatever limitations they must accept, can at least converse with their fellows and establish the human contacts which happy life demands. . . . What we can do for the deaf in the way of training, education and practical help can be nullified unless they are taught also to live with their handicap among hearing people and unless hearing people are also taught to live with the deaf' (Kershaw, 1961). How can this be achieved?

To begin with, it is vital that assessment and education begin at the earliest possible moment, which means the first year of life. Whatever the cause and type of deafness, if there is any useful hearing, the child must learn to listen and to associate sounds with meaning. Hearing aids can and should be used by children a few months old and if worn constantly, they grow accustomed to them more quickly than 3- to 5-year-olds. During the first two years, the mother plays a most important part. It is primarily she who carries out the necessary auditory training, who ensures that her child has constant practice in listening and who, with the professional help of trained staff, guides his early speech development. In some areas home teachers are employed to support the family during the preschool years and then to provide a link between home and school. Special nursery units for giving auditory training to the preschool child, preferably in a day setting, are also available in some parts of the country.

When school age is reached, there is little doubt that the profoundly deaf child will need the expert teaching techniques and the technical equipment, such as loop amplifiers, which only a special school can

provide. Those whose hearing is impaired may do best in units for
the partially hearing attached to ordinary schools; these have the
advantage that the handicapped child can spend part of the day with
normal children to the benefit of both. Since such units are a comparatively recent venture, many hearing impaired children are likely to
attend a special school for the partially deaf unless they can cope in an
ordinary school.

4. Education in living with a handicap

To be handicapped is to belong to a minority group. This always poses
some problems of relationships: being unable to do and to live like the
majority creates a sense of isolation; consciousness of being different
makes the handicapped person awkward or shy which calls out similar
reactions in the normal. Moreover, few of the non-handicapped majority
are completely at ease in the company of the handicapped. In addition
to general unease, different handicaps evoke different emotional
responses. Blindness evokes the most favourable and the most universally
compassionate attitudes; pity and admiration are readily extended to
child and adult alike, as is a helping hand.

Towards the deaf there is an almost diametrically opposed attitude:
intolerance, irritation, and even ridicule are widespread. At best the
deaf are tactfully avoided, partly because trying to communicate with
them is slow and cumbersome, and partly because the non-handicapped
feel embarrassed having to repeat things and to shout when doing so;
even then misunderstandings occur readily and are difficult to sort out.
Moreover, this irritation and embarrassment communicates itself to the
deaf so that they in turn become embarrassed, anxious or aggressive,
according to temperament. The fact that it is an 'invisible' handicap
which the sufferer may try to conceal just because of the response it
evokes, only makes the situation worse.

Attitudes towards physical disabilities vary widely, covering the
whole range of emotions from sympathy to ridicule; the limbless are
pitied while the stammerer is mimicked. Visibility (i.e. how obvious)
and appearance (i.e. how ugly or malformed) also influence the degree
of acceptance or tolerance.

Towards children these general attitudes are usually modified by a
protective pity. While this shields them during their most vulnerable
years, at the same time it must make their entry into the adult world a
baffling and painful, if not traumatic, experience. A sympathetic,
compassionate and often over-protective world inexplicably turns into
one of embarrassed, evasive and irritated people. This may lead some
handicapped young people to self-pity as well as to seeking to evoke

pity; others may withdraw into the world of the handicapped or the protection of their family or into their own inner world; still others may grow to resent and fight their disability in an attempt to lead an even more 'normal' life than the non-handicapped.

Education in living with a handicap must have its roots in a deliberate and realistic appraisal of the possible. In the first place this has to be made for the young child jointly by all those concerned for his care, management and education. It begins in the home and for many years to come parents will provide this education. Meeting the child's basic emotional needs in appropriate ways is one part of this education; gradually teaching the child a clearsighted acceptance of possibilities (and inevitable limitations) is another; helping him through periods of resentment, bitterness, apathy and despair is perhaps the most difficult and painful part when parental hopes and ambitions have also been shattered. A consoling, healing and encouraging experience for parent and child is to meet similarly handicapped children and adults, both those struggling like themselves and those who have successfully faced or, better still, triumphed over equal or worse obstacles. Knowing what can be achieved helps to maintain high but realistic standards as well as high morale.

There are two criteria by which successful adaptation to handicap is judged in adult life: the ability to earn a living; and the ability to live an independent life. Both of these are big aims and in pursuing them it is easy to overlook that the little things of life may have a disproportionate effect in both areas, just because they happen all the time. For example, an invalid car or wheelchair may be essential for getting about and neither needs to curtail independence seriously; but requiring constant help with feeding or toileting not only makes for much greater dependence but it is infinitely more embarrasing. Thus, developing self-help in matters of cleanliness, personal hygiene and neatness deserve the greatest perseverance. Time and energy devoted to their achievement by home and school will pay good dividends later. The fullest use should be made too of any aids, gadgets and new devices which come on the market; also there are many little tricks or hints which assist in learning and managing everyday activities. Many children will pick these up incidentally by watching others or discovering them for themselves. But all who have had experience in caring and educating the handicapped have a fund of such techniques; if they are passed on to children (and their parents) to learn during the formative years it can avoid a lot of useless or wrong learning.

Another important aspect of living with a handicap is the ability to accept help gracefully as well as to invite it when required. This needs to be taught alongside the need for independence. Normal people are unnecessarily made to feel rebuffed when a well-meant offer of help is brusquely rejected. How to reject and how to invite help is an art worth mastering as is the understanding when to accept it for the sake of the would-be helper, even when assistance is not in fact needed.

Education for recreation comes a close second to education for employment. Hobbies, the various arts, games such as chess or cards, and also certain physical sports may well be within the child's capacity; indeed, some, like music or swimming, can be of therapeutic value. Not only do recreational pursuits provide bridges to the world of the non-handicapped; they also provide opportunities to make relations with the opposite sex during adolescence, when most young people are looking for romance and eventually marriage. This is a particularly neglected aspect of education in living with a handicap, probably because it is so fraught with hurt, damaged self-esteem and, most important of all, because there are no easy or ready answers. All this, every handicapped young person must face sooner or later; if he can do so with the help of a compassionate, understanding and honest adult, then his (and even more so her) learning will be that much less difficult. Getting to know handicapped people who have made successful marriages may give hope. For some, marriage may be a very unlikely goal; the knowledge that some people are successfully and happily wedded to their work or hobby may be a consolation and aim for them.

2. Aims and Methods

1. How the study came about

Ever since the first children damaged by the drug thalidomide were born, intense public attention has been focused on the victims as well as on the general medical and social aspects of the tragedy. As a result, there is more public understanding of the nature of the resulting defects and greater sympathy than for many other types of handicapping conditions. It is estimated that between 1959 and 1962 some 500 children with limb and other deficiencies resulting from thalidomide were born in Britain. Chief among the organisations concerned for their care and campaigning for better provision of all kinds is the Lady Hoare Thalidomide Appeal. At first, the Appeal concentrated on the provision of adequate medical and limb-fitting services, together with social work support and welfare assistance for the families. Then, as the first children started to attend school, attention was directed to their educational needs and to whether adequate provision was available for them now and in the foreseeable future.

To investigate this question, Lady Hoare invited the National Bureau for Co-operation in Child Care to undertake this enquiry, the field work for which began in January 1968.

There has been a great deal of discussion whether children affected by the drug have unique problems which require consideration on a national level; or whether only some of them have very specific needs while others do not; or whether limb deficiences caused by thalidomide present a range of difficulties not markedly different from similar physical handicaps due to other factors. In short, do 'thalidomide children' have unique educational needs or not? To try to answer this question, it was decided to carry out a pilot study in an area of the country which contained a comparatively high incidence of cases which were geographically fairly compact. Eventually Scotland was chosen for this purpose.

2. How the children were located

The starting point in locating the children was a list kept by the Lady Hoare Thalidomide Appeal. Its Social Welfare Officer supplied names of fifty-three children whose families she had visited on one or more occasion. Then the Scottish Education Department was approached and made available to the study a list of children known to it in April 1967. A year later a revised and supplemented list was brought out containing 118 children. The existence of all three lists was invaluable in building up our sample without too much delay. However, none of them was complete. While the Appeal's list contained less than half the children on the government department's list, the latter omitted some eight cases known to the Appeal, whose authenticity was not in doubt. In addition, further enquiries revealed that the much longer official lists included limb-deficient children who were not genuine thalidomide cases though their defects were congenital in origin.

The question then arose whether the study should be confined to 'authentic' cases and how these could be defined. Even a few of the fifty-three mothers on the Thalidomide Appeal's list declared categorically that they took no drugs whatever during pregnancy, while many more were uncertain whether they took any tablets and if so, which. 'I was that sick, my doctor tried all sorts; he tried to trace them afterwards but couldn't be sure' was a typical comment. On what grounds might one identify an 'authentic' thalidomide child?

Sometimes all the evidence was positive: accurate medical records were available, the child had the most recognisable forms of defect, the mother confirmed that she had taken a certain drug and the child's name was on the lists of both the Scottish Education Department and of the Charitable Trust. Occasionally one of those conditions was not met, but on balance the evidence was positive on all counts in sixty cases; it was rather doubtful in nine cases; and definitely negative in eleven cases – that is mother, medical records and physical features all indicated that the defect was not caused by this drug though the child's name appeared on the Scottish Education Department's list. Three of these eleven children were clearly too old: one was approaching ten and the other two were both $13\frac{1}{2}$ years old. However, since their parents accepted the general invitation to co-operate in the survey, they were assessed on such of the tests as were appropriate in the hope of obtaining perhaps a few pointers about later development, adaptation and difficulties which might help towards assessing thalidomide problems. In fact, these three cases were too disparate for this purpose. There is, however, little doubt that a survey of a bigger comparative sample, extended to other physically defective groups, would yield very useful information.

In addition to some of the above nine 'doubtfuls', who are probably 'genuine', and at least some of the 'refusals' and the 'failures to respond', there are probably still a few completely unknown cases, such as one child reported by another parent where the mother had said that her child couldn't be included because she obtained pills from a chemist and not her doctor.

All told, the available evidence suggests that a total of around eighty 'authentic' cases in Scotland is a realistic estimate, in which case our sample of sixty children amounts to about 75 per cent of all likely cases. This group will from now on be referred to as 'authentic' thalidomide children but, of course, in this context the term carries no legal implications; nor is it in the nature of a medically undisputed diagnosis. Moreover, for the purpose of the survey, there seemed no reason why one need differentiate between a child born with an arm stump rounded off and one with the typical inward twist and vestigial fingers. So it was decided to contact all possible cases and offer them the opportunity to participate in the enquiry.

The children on the Scottish Education Department's list were traced through the Directors of Education. On informing them of the study and in seeking their permission to contact schools, they were asked also for the address of any such child said to live in their area.

When information concerning the whereabouts of the total group became available, the vast majority was found to live in the central industrial belt between and around Edinburgh and Glasgow. It was, therefore, decided to make the headquarters in Edinburgh and to carry out as many examinations there as possible. Because all the children had had so much hospital experience, it seemed desirable to avoid this setting and to provide instead premises more akin to the classroom of an infant's school. Premises which the university agreed to make available proved very suitable for the purpose; they consisted of an ordinary terrace house, some 10 minutes from the central railway station, which helped to keep journeys to the minimum.

Those living in Aberdeen and in the Inverness area were interviewed in their own schools or in premises made available by the Child Guidance Clinic in Aberdeen. For parents who had difficulty in arranging transport themselves or who wished to have an escort, the W.R.V.S. provided whatever was required.

Of the total of 118 children eventually traced, 81 were individually interviewed and tested. The remaining 37 could not be seen for a variety of reasons (Table 1). Refusals to co-operate amounted to some 26 per cent among the available 109 children still living in Scotland. One child, who was examined but subsequently excluded from the

Table 1 Reasons why not interviewed $(N = 38)$

Reasons	Numbers
Left Scotland	9
Failed to respond	16
Refused to take part	6
Failed to keep repeated appointments	4
None of several appointments offered suitable	2
Excluded from final analysis though seen	1

analysis, turned out to have been an accident victim when aged about $3\frac{1}{2}$ years. Of the fifty-three cases on the Lady Hoare Thalidomide Fund's list, forty-six or 87 per cent were seen; of the seven children whose families failed to co-operate, at least three were reported to be severely handicapped. Of the sixty-five children traced with the help of government departments thirty-four or 52 per cent were interviewed. Why the refusal rate in this group should have been so much higher than in the other is a matter for conjecture. Might it be that the same circumstances were operative which decided them against seeking the help and advice of the Lady Hoare Thalidomide Appeal? The nature of these circumstances could well range from the determination or the ability to manage unaided, down to apathy or rejection.

Both parents were invited to bring the child and in about half the cases both did in fact come along for the interview. For the remainder, the mother came alone or, in five cases, accompanied by an older relative. In the few instances where no relative at all was seen, information was provided by professional workers, such as doctors, teachers, housemothers and matrons. In 90 per cent of the cases one or both parents were interviewed (Table 2).

Table 2 Adults who accompanied the child $(N = 80)$

	Numbers
Both parents	37
Mother only (5 with relatives)	35
Father only	2
Grandmother only	1
No relative	5

3. The assessment procedures[1]

To establish how well the children were responding to the educational opportunities available to them and, in turn, how suitable these appeared

[1] All the interviewing, testing and other field work was carried out by one of the authors (D.O.F.)

in the light of a particular child's developmental pattern, as comprehensive an assessment as possible was carried out. This involved testing general ability by both verbal and non-verbal means; gathering information on current educational achievements; and obtaining a picture of the social and emotional behaviour shown both at home and at school. Altogether some ten different tests and assessments were used, supplemented by interviewing the child and one or both of his parents.

Needless to say, some of the tests required a degree of manual dexterity and motor control which was beyond the capabilities of a limb-deficient child. This was not only inevitable but an essential part of the procedure. Only by observing how the children coped in strictly standard situations could one judge how they compared with their contemporaries and thus the extent to which allowances would have to be made if they were expected to hold their own in ordinary schools. This meant that in some cases certain tests or some part of them had to be omitted, such as verbal items when a profoundly deaf child was being examined.

Information was drawn from three main sources: the children themselves, their parents and their teachers. Additionally, reports were made available by the Lady Hoare Thalidomide Appeal's social welfare worker on the cases known to her.

The first half hour or so was spent talking to the parents while the child was given an opportunity to get used to his surroundings and to become at ease by having toys and other equipment put at his disposal. During this time a brief history was obtained as well as an account of the child's behaviour at home and of the family's hopes and ambitions for his future. The primary aim was to obtain a developmental history of the child and not the social history of the family.

Each child was then individually interviewed. Since this assessment took from 1 hour to $2\frac{1}{2}$ hours, depending on his ability to cope and to persevere, it was also possible to gain some insight into his attitudes and adjustment; whether he was confident or very dependent on praise and encouragement; whether he persevered in the face of difficulty or too readily gave up trying; whether he formed a friendly relationship with a strange though sympathetic adult, or remained wary, withdrawn or altogether hostile. Breaks for toileting, drinks and biscuits provided an opportunity for observing the child's ability to look after himself and also to watch how he was using the available play materials.

All the tests and procedures chosen for this study are well-known (and, where appropriate, standardised) instruments, widely used for the educational and psychological assessment of children, both normal and those who have special needs (a detailed list is given in Appendix A). Between them, they tap a wide range of abilities, skills and attainments, such as the level of spoken and written vocabulary, reasoning ability, power of recalled span of attention, visual discrimination, hand–eye co-ordination, literacy and numeracy.

In additon, teachers were asked to complete a detailed assessment schedule on the child's behaviour at school in relation not only to his teacher but also to his classmates. Two items requiring the teacher to rate (on a four point scale from 'very good' to 'quite incompetent') the child's level of work in English and arithmetic were included.

Thus the information collected fell into three parts: aspects of performance and behaviour which were measured; attitudes which were observed or inferred; and descriptive accounts given by those closely concerned and familiar with the child in the everyday context of home and school.

The tabulated results are given at the end of the book to avoid constantly interrupting the flow of the text. There the statistically interested reader can see the evidence on which the major conclusions are based. Calculations have been confined to the very simplest, namely averages and percentages. No tests of statistical significance were carried out as they would be inappropriate or even misleading for a population so small and so heterogeneous as our group.

Individual reports were prepared on each child to show his level of intellectual ability and educational attainments and to describe his personality strength and weaknesses; the appropriateness of present schooling and likely needs at the secondary stage were also discussed. These reports were given to the parents, the Appeal and the Scottish Education Department. A number of these are shown in Appendix H.

3. Findings for the Whole Group

Of the eighty children seen, thirty-seven were boys and forty-three girls. The great majority (seventy-seven or 96 per cent) were within the age range of $4\frac{1}{2}$ to $8\frac{1}{2}$ years. The remaining three cases were 'over age' girls (i.e. born before 1959) who had been taken from the Scottish Education Department's list (Table 3). There was a higher proportion

Table 3. Age range

Age range	Boys N	Girls N	Total N	%
4 yr 8 mth to 5 yr 5 mth	5	2	7	8
5 yr 6 mth to 7 yr 5 mth	28	31	59	74
7 yr 6 mth to 9 yr	4	7	11	14
Above 9 yr	—	3	3	4

of boys among the youngest children, whereas girls predominated among the oldest. About a quarter of the goup (nineteen or 24 per cent) were of approximately the same age as those in the National Child Development Study (1958 Cohort) and thus their educational attainments were directly comparable.

1. Range, degree and type of defects

There was a wide range of physical defects and deformities, from a child without a left thumb to those who were virtually limbless; and from a child with one or two minor defects, such as a foreshortened, twisted or misshapen leg, as well as impaired hearing, to those with very severe and multiple deformities (Table 4). An attempt was made to apply a fivefold classification to the degree of damage so that comparisons could be made between the intellectual and educational functioning of severely, moderately and minimally damaged children respectively. This was by no means easy since there are no objective criteria to enable

Table 4 The nature of the defects*

	No. of children
Limb deficiencies: $N = 59$	
Severe limb deficiencies: both arms and legs	9
Severe upper-limb deficiencies: no arms, or very short and twisted	28
Severe lower-limb deficiencies: virtually no legs	4
Unilateral: defect of one arm or one leg–arm: 14	
leg: 4	18
Auditory defects (actual or suspected): $N = 20$	
No external ears and/or deformities of the inner ear sufficient to cause profound hearing impairment (of this group 12 had only one ear)	13
Impaired hearing suspected	7
Visual defects (some not due to thalidomide): $N = 18$	
4 of these were severe	18
Others: $N = 19$	
Facial paralysis and speech defects	4
Bowel and other internal deformities	7
Speech defects, in addition to the inevitable language difficulties of deaf children	8

* These are not mutually exclusive so that the total number of defects is greater than the number of children.

such judgments to be made. For example, is a missing thumb, because of its effect on grasping, a greater or lesser handicap than a twisted ankle which affects gait; and does the more immediate or marked visibility of the latter add an emotional overlay which is absent from the relatively minor visual impact of the former? There was the further complication that many other defects were present in addition to limb deficiencies. Hence any classification is bound to be arbitrary. Moreover, a comparatively mild physical defect resulting in only slight functional impairment may have a profoundly handicapping effect psychologically on a particular individual. The attempt to assess the degree of impairment for our sample indicated that over a third of the children were severely disabled and about a third were moderately affected while the remainder had suffered relatively slight damage only (Table 5). Though all the children in the 'doubtful' and 'non-thalido-mide' groups had limb deficiencies of various kinds, the degree and extent of impairment were much milder.

The most severe degree of damage was among the 'authentic' thalido-mide cases. Of those with severe defects, five children were virtually limbless and seven had no external ears except for 'fleshy buttons', as

Table 5 Degree of damage

Degree	Authentic cases $N = 60$	Doubtful $N = 9$	Non-thalidomide $N = 11$	Total N	%
Very severe defect	12 } 38%	—	1	13	16
Severe defect	11	—	—	11	14
Moderate defect	20 33%	—	2	22	28
Slight/mild defect	13 } 28%	2	2	17	21
Minimal defect	4	7	6	17	21

well as deformities of the inner ear resulting in profound deafness. Surgical intervention had generally been unsuccessful in making artificial channels. The earless children also tended to have some facial paralysis or a deformity of the mouth, accompanied by articulation difficulties; squints too were in evidence, further detracting from their appearance.

Another twelve children had less severe auditory defects or were at least suspected of suffering some hearing impairment. Thus no fewer than a third of the 'authentic' thalidomide cases were affected by some auditory loss, which in many cases was very severe.

Defective eyesight affected about a quarter of the children though thalidomide may not always have been responsible. Nearly 10 per cent were or had been afflicted with bowel or other internal deformities. All these defects were additional to limb deficiencies of various degrees of severity, for which, moreover, many children had had operations; among these were the removal of extra digits from hands or feet, and the straightening or strengthening of twisted wrists or ankles. In many cases there was a need for further surgical intervention to correct deformities or to make thumbs or ear channels; and also for the continued provision of artificial aids of one kind or another.

Of the 'authentic' cases, almost half had either no arms or very short, twisted ones with the typical thalidomide vestigial fingers or flipper-limbs; additionally, 25 per cent had one deformed arm. Five children had virtually no legs or arms and a further four had all limbs affected though not to such a severe degree; thus altogether 15 per cent had defects of both arms and legs.

From an educational point of view, sensory defects and deformities of the upper limbs are clearly more handicapping than lower limb damage, even though limited mobility and inability to participate in physical activities inevitably restrict a child's capacity to play a full part in the life of an ordinary school. With regard to sensory handicaps, there is little doubt that severely impaired hearing is more detrimental to intellectual, educational and social development than visual defects. Moreover, while seven children were profoundly deaf, none was totally blind.

2. Intellectual and language development

Of the four tests used for the assessment of general ability, two were verbal and two non-verbal. The overall results from each were very similar, and broadly comparable to those obtained from the general child population. Also the findings for the various sub-groups were remarkably similar (Appendix B). For this reason, the children's general intellectual functioning will be described only with regard to the Terman–Merrill Scale, which is the most generally applied test of its kind. The present level of general intellectual functioning for the whole group of eighty children was found to be about average. As one would predict, those minimally damaged have the highest average score, while those whose disabilities were very severe, scored lowest. However, overall the latter were found to be within the average range for general ability. The only exception were children with hearing impairment, but this was to some extent a reflection of the assessment procedure itself which did not include tests specifically designed for those so affected.

The range and distribution of intellectual functioning among the whole group of children were also comparable with those existing in the general population. Thus about a quarter were found to be of superior or very superior general ability and a very similar proportion were at the opposite end of the scale, namely dull or very dull; about half the children fell into the average band (I.Q. 85 to 115). Excluding those with impaired hearing, measured quotients on this test ranged from 60 to 145, i.e. from educationally subnormal to potential university calibre (Table 6).

Table 6 Terman–Merrill Intelligence Quotients Distribution

	Very able	Superior	Average	Dull	Educationally subnormal
I.Q. range	130+	115–130	85–115	70–85	70 and below
Number	5	15	42	11	7
Percentage	6	19	53	13	9

Looking at level of intellectual functioning in relation to type of school, fee-paying pupils were found to have the highest average score (Mean Terman I.Q. 119), next came those attending state primary schools (Mean Terman I.Q. 106) and the lowest level of intellectual functioning prevailed among those in schools for the physically handicapped (Mean Terman I.Q. 94·5). An interpretation of the meaning of these findings will be made later in the light of parental attitudes, the schools' standards of expectation and the degree of the child's handicap (pp. 33–36 and Chapter 6).

On the non-verbal tests, the findings were broadly similar. An average score was made by the group as a whole; again, pupils at fee-paying schools did better than those attending state primary schools and the latter did better than pupils at special schools (Appendix B). On all measures, children with minimal physical impairment did better than those where it was severe (Table 7).

Table 7 Mean I.Q.s in relation to degree of physical impairment, thalidomide only (excluding 7 deaf)

Test	Mild (Grades I and II) $N = 17$	Moderate (Grade III) $N = 20$	Severe (Grades IV and V) $N = 16$
Terman–Merrill	109	98	97
English Picture Vocabulary	105	99	99
Raven's Matrices	102	91	98
Goodenough Draw-a-man	98	83	82

3. Educational attainments

It must be borne in mind that the great majority were still in the infant stage of education (i.e. 83 per cent were below the age of $7\frac{1}{2}$ years). At that time one would expect that a sizeable minority of normal children would only just have made a beginning with formal, measurable attainment. This would inevitably be the case to a much greater extent among a group of handicapped children, if for no other reason than that most of the earliest learning of the handicapped preschool child is bound to be adversely affected by his disability; hence he will be less ready for the more formal learning expected of him when he starts attending school. The need for hospital treatment would also have a detrimental effect on school attendance.

Educational attainments were assessed by two means; standardised achievement tests and according to judgments made by teachers of their pupils' educational level. It was confined to the two subjects of particular relevance during a child's primary schooling, namely reading and arithmetic.

Reading. About half the group had achieved a reading level average or above average for their age. One of the highest achievers was an exceptionally intelligent 6-year-old girl who reached a ten-year level, both in comprehension and accuracy. As expected, all the very good readers were children of above average ability.

About a quarter of the group had not yet acquired sufficient reading skills to allow for assessments to be made with standardised tests. Since some twenty-four of the children were less than 6 years old, one could hardly expect them as yet to have achieved much more than being able to cope with pre-reading material. The proportion of poor readers was considerably higher among pupils attending special schools – 50 per cent compared with only 20 per cent among those in ordinary schools. In view of the fact that it tends to be the more severely disabled who attend special schools of one kind or another, this was quite predictable. Profoundly deaf children, have been excluded here since their scholastic progress, particularly in linguistic skills, is bound to be severely prejudiced by the very nature of their handicap.

According to the teachers' assessments, some 30 per cent of children were backward in this subject. On the other hand, a similar proportion (33 per cent) were described as good readers. A comparison between the reading attainment of a normal national sample of 7-year-olds,[1] as judged by their teachers on the same assessment schedule (Stott), shows just how satisfactory a reading level this group of thalidomide children has achieved: the overall proportion of good, average and poor readers respectively is very similar indeed for the handicapped and the normal group (Table 8).

Table 8 Comparative reading ability

Teachers' ratings	Thalidomide (%)	National sample[1] (%)
Good	33	30
Average	37	43
Poor	23	23
Non-readers	7	3

Arithmetic. A somewhat higher proportion were found to be backward in arithmetic both according to test results and in the teachers' opinion who judged some 39 per cent to be backward. Comparisons are also available here with the normal sample of 7-year-old children. Twice as many thalidomide children received very low scores, and conversely, only half

[1] The National Child Development Study (1958 Cohort); quoted in *11,000 Seven-year-olds*, Pringle, Butler and Davie, Longmans, 1966.

as many achieved high scores (Table 9). Again, the children attending ordinary schools consistently achieved higher scores than those in special schools.

Table 9 Comparative arithmetic test performance

Test score	Thalidomide (%)	National sample* (%)
0–3	60	29
4–6	25	41
6–10	15	30

* The National Child Development Study (1958 Cohort); quoted in *11,000 Seven-year-olds*. Pringle, Butler and Davie, Longmans, 1966.

4. Social and emotional adjustment

Information on the children's personal and behavioural characteristics was culled from three sources: the psychologist's observations of the child during the more formal part of the interview when the various tests were administered, as well as during the periods of spontaneous play; the information volunteered by the parents supplemented by that elicited through direct questioning; and an account of the child's behaviour in school, both in relation to his teacher and his classmates, obtained by using the Bristol Social Adjustment Guides. The last mentioned were available for all but two children, both of whom can be regarded as being well-adjusted according to all other information about them.

There was close agreement between the observations made during the psychological interview and the teachers' assessments provided by the Guides. In only two cases did notable discrepancies occur: in the one, the child was reported to show no signs whatever of maladjustment in school but during the interview he exhibited clear signs of stress and tension; his home circumstances were such that it was in no way surprising to find him under such emotional strain. The other child seemed to have 'got across' her teacher so much that it was evident from the report that nothing she did would ever be right or please her teacher. This child co-operated very well during the interview; and though the home circumstances were not those of an ordinary family, at the same time she was being given thoughtful and loving care by her guardians.

The majority of children were judged to be 'stable' while about one in eight (13 per cent) showed symptoms of maladjustment. Comparison with the large scale National Child Development Study (1958 Cohort) indicates that the incidence of problem behaviour is very similar. Because the age ranges are not strictly comparable (all the normal children were 7 years old whereas the range among our sample was from $4\frac{1}{2}$ to $8\frac{1}{2}$) one can only draw tentative conclusions. However, these suggest that though many of our children had severe physical and sensory disabilities, emotional maladjustment was no more prevalent among them than among the non-handicapped.

Analysing the relative incidence of emotional difficulties among boys and girls separately, an interesting difference emerges in comparison with the national sample. Whereas among this normal group, there were twice as many maladjusted boys as girls, in the case of the thalidomide group there were more maladjusted girls (Table 10).

Table 10 Adjustment of the thalidomide sample compared with the national cohort

| | Thalidomide | | | National Cohort | | |
	Boys	Girls	Both	Boys	Girls	Both
Stable	68%	54%	60%	60%	74%	64%
Unsettled	21%	32%	27%	25%	18%	23%
Maladjusted	12%	14%	13%	16%	8%	13%

The symptoms most frequently reported for the thalidomide sample were 'anxiety or uncertainty about adult interest and affection', followed closely by 'restlessness' – which is thought to be an avoidance response to acute anxiety – and 'unforthcomingness' – which is defined as a lack of confidence before any new or difficult situation, together with lack of assertiveness and curiosity. Next in frequency came 'depression', then a 'writing-off or unconcern for adult approval' and next 'hostility to children and adults'. Thus the evidence suggests that at this age the most common emotional response to the stressful reality of handicap is a deep concern and fear about adult love and acceptance; in about a quarter of the whole group this was a marked feature but this same anxiety was felt to a lesser extent by one in every two children.

Looking at the pattern of emotional disturbance in relation to age, the most seriously affected seemed to be those aged between 6 and $6\frac{1}{2}$ years. In relation to the severity of the physical impairment, the most severely disabled are not necessarily the most disturbed emotionally, and vice versa. A brief description of the most seriously disturbed children may serve to illustrate this point.

(a) The child rated the most seriously maladjusted was earless and deaf, with facial paralysis and communication difficulties; he had no parents.

(b) The next most disturbed was moderately limb deficient (one leg only affected), suspected of some hearing impairment and of limited intellectual capacity; he was attending a special school; his father was said to be indifferent to the child.

(c) The next was of average intelligence; with very short arms, attending an ordinary school; severe academic pressure from parents.

(d) Then there was a bright child attending a fee-paying school; the physical defects were very minor but an emotional disturbance in the mother seemed to be reflected in the child's behaviour.

Now to turn to observations made during the psychological examination. Considering the children's age, they seemed to show greater social confidence, poise and verbal precocity than expected, particularly in view of the fact that they came predominantly from lower-middle-class and working-class families. They were neither sorry for themselves nor did they unduly anticipate failure. The most minimally defective appeared to be the most aware of their deficiency. There were fewer children within the average range of emotional maturity: they seemed to be either markedly dependent or markedly independent of adult help. All gave the impression of being aware of the fact that they were objects of public interest and concern. Might this have something to do with their social poise as well as the fact that frequent visits to hospitals and clinics have made them come into contact with a wide range of people, most of whom also extend to them this concerned interest and compassion?

An analysis of the children's choice of future occupation revealed an overwhelming preference among girls to be a nurse and among boys to be a doctor. No doubt this is, at least in part, a reflection of their close and continued contact with these professions. Otherwise, occupational choices were very similar to those made by ordinary children of this age, including the same juxtaposition of rather divergent careers such as 'a doctor or a hairdresser'. One little girl longed to be a ballet dancer but reasoned that this was impractical 'because of my hands'. Another insisted firmly that, like her mummy, she would 'do nothing'. Teaching, secretarial work and becoming a 'police lady' all featured in the girls' replies. The boys, on the other hand, favoured more active, outdoor pursuits such as becoming a builder, milk roundsman, taxi driver, fireman, policeman and a Rentokil man (after his father).

Needless to say one does not expect a reliable or realistic vocational preference from such young children. Rather, occupational advice is used as a further means of gaining insight into the child's feelings and thoughts.

5. Home background and parental attitudes

Socio-economic level. The majority of the families came from social class II, III and IV (according to the Registrar General's classification), the greater number belonging to the lower end of the socio-economic scale. A few children came from vulnerable or socially deprived families, where low income, unemployment or the loss of the breadwinner were causing not only financial hardship but also emotional stress. One child from a tinker family had had to be taken into the care of the local authority. At the other end of the scale, there was one solicitor's child and one father was a company director. None came from families which expect their children to be educated at a British type public school as a matter of course.

Social histories were not systematically taken nor was the information from the Fund's Welfare Officer uniform or complete in every case. Hence no further generalisations can justifiably be made.

Position in family. Some thirty children were, at the time of the survey, the youngest in their family and possibly would be the last. Three of these came from large families and were said to be doted on by their older siblings. The number of first-borns was also thirty. Of these, twenty-four were the oldest of two, three or four siblings. There were six only children. One of these had been rejected by parents who were separating; another (non-thalidomide) child had very severe and multiple defects and the parents said that they had made a deliberate decision not to have any more children.

There were known to be three sets of twins. One pair of girls was rather dissimilar and the affected twin, who was of average ability, was said to be outstripping her sister in many ways. In the second set, the damaged twin was an earless, very severely handicapped and retarded child whose twin brother was reported to be quite normal and of average ability. The third set, twin boys both of whom were affected, was not seen as the parents failed to respond to all approaches.

Two of the children had been adopted. In one case there were four older, natural children, three of whom were married; in the other case there were no other children in the adoptive family.

A few of the mothers explicitly expressed the fear that the handicapped child might, at some later stage, become a burden to brothers or sisters. In two or three cases this was linked with a determination to provide or obtain whatever financial and social support might be needed to ensure that other siblings would not be penalised.

Parental hopes and ambitions. Inevitably, the long-term prospects of their children had been considered by most parents, even though the majority agreed that it was far too early to think in terms of vocational training or employment. By far the commonest hope and wish was that the child should eventually be capable of leading an independent life and of earning his living. There was parental preference for non-manual, professional work. A frequent and quite reasonable argument in the circumstances was that 'he won't be able to use his hands, so he will have to rely on his brain'. Partly for this reason education was seen to be of immense importance.

Staying on at school and getting as many certificates and diplomas as possible was seen as highly desirable. Several parents hoped that a university education would be possible. While it is recognised that parental ambition is a powerful motivating force for children, it is perhaps a little disquieting that very few parents questioned whether their handicapped child would find it impossible to reach the necessary academic standards. Perhaps this reflects the Scottish tradition of high educational expectations. Conversely, quite a number of parents had very decided views about their child's future career even though most were not yet 8 years old. Clearly an over-ambitious attitude may well lead to undue and possibly harmful pressure on the child; while an unrealistically optimistic outlook could lead to painful disappointments, for both the child and the parents.

In one instance this was already happening and the child in question was showing markedly unfavourable emotional reactions in response to very over-demanding parental ambitions.

Stability of home background and emotional climate. There were overtly stressful circumstances in at least a quarter of the families; it is very likely that this is a minimum estimate since there was little direct questioning. In some cases stress was due to recognised overt disturbance in one or both parents; in others it was the relationship between different members of the family, but primarily between the parents themselves, or between them and the child which were very disturbed. In yet others, additional hardship, including adverse social conditions and severe cultural deprivation, were affecting the family. The unfavourable circumstances present covered a wide range of economically and emotionally stressful conditions (Table 11).

In the cases with divorced parents, one child had a stepfather; a second was living with her mother and relatives; the third was partially rejected by the deserted mother and placed in care. Of the children living in residential care one was in a subnormality hospital and rejected by his divorced parents; the second was rejected by his natural mother who herself was under psychiatric care; and the third came from a tinker family and was taken into care because of neglect.

Table 11 Stressful conditions

Conditions	Numbers
Father deceased; children profoundly deaf	2
No father because of divorce	3
Illegitimate, 'in care' and eventually adopted	2
Child living in residential care	4
One parent receiving psychiatric treatment	4
Father unemployed	3
Father in prison	2

Additionally, many mothers reported that at some time during the child's life they had had treatment for 'nerves' either from a general practitioner or in hospital. A great many had, of course, been given a prescription in the first place for 'nerves', depression, sleeplessness or sickness, not necessarily directly attributable to acknowledged pregnancy; some mothers had had depression or other disturbances in the early stages after the baby's birth and some were still 'on pills'. Others, overtly healthy, declared that they would 'never get over it' or have 'never been the same since'.

6. Achievement and adjustment in relation to physical impairment and environmental circumstances

Composite ratings. In an attempt to arrive at an overall assessment of each child's all-round disability a composite global rating score was worked out. This was done by assigning to each of the five aspects which were explored a numerical score, 1 representing the optimal and 5 the most serious condition. Hence, a high level of intellectual functioning, high educational achievement, good emotional or social adjustment, favourable environmental circumstances and minimal physical impairment each would be given a score of one, resulting, by addition, in a composite score of five; conversely, a score of five in each of the five areas would denote the least favourable situation, resulting in a composite score of 25.

The following aspects were combined to make up the composite score:

1. Intellectual assessment – combined results from four tests.
2. Educational attainment – combined results from five tests and teachers' assessments.
3. Emotional/social adjustment – combined results from the Bristol Social Adjustment Guides, observations of and interview with child and parents.

4. Physical impairment – assessed on a five point scale.
5. Environmental circumstances – combining home background, parental attitudes and educational facilities.

To give two hypothetical examples from the extreme ends of the
composite scale: an able child who is making excellent progress at
school, is well-adjusted and sociable, has only a minor physical deformity
such as a twisted left hand, and comes from a good home where material
conditions are satisfactory and where the family is accepting and supportive in its attitude – such a child would receive a score of 5. On the
other hand, a child receiving a composite score of 25 would be grossly
disabled, possibly without limbs or with severe sensory impairment, who
is mentally subnormal, educationally severely backward, emotionally
and socially seriously disturbed; whose parents are inadequate, the father
being an alcoholic and the mother psychiatrically ill, both being unable
to cope with life in general and their handicapped child in particular, and who finally reject him so that he has to be taken into residential
care. Such a child clearly has few resources in his endowment, his environment or in himself because of gross deprivations of several kinds from
the earliest stage of his life; hence from the outset he is not only physically but also emotionally and intellectually damaged and inadequate.

So at the extremes, there is on the one hand the near-normal, optimally
favoured child, and on the other hand, the grossly handicapped and
deprived child. It could be argued that to some extent the factor of
thalidomide is of relatively marginal significance in such cases and also
that there are equally handicapped children whose condition is due to
circumstances other than the drug.

It was hoped that this composite indicator might be useful in a number
of ways: it would show the extent of the difficulties faced by each child;
it would be possible at one glance to single out those with the most
serious problems; and it would allow comparisons to be made between
particular groups of children.

The overall picture. To summarise the picture which emerged, the composite score for each of our eighty children (Appendix E, p. 80) was
divided into three equal parts: 5 to 11 = relatively mildly affected;
12 to 18 = considerably affected; 19 to 25 = very severely affected.
There are some twelve children in the last category; deafness and rejection are the salient characteristics of this group, three of whom are
also severely limb-deficient. In the second category there are thirty-six
cases, who show a wide range of handicapping conditions; and for the
remainder, some thirty-two children, the overall picture shows the
adverse conditions to be relatively mild (Table 12).

Table 12 Summary of composite scores

Very severely affected (score of 19–25)	$N = 12$ (15%)
Considerably affected (score 12–18)	$N = 36$ (45%)
Relatively mildly affected (score 5–11)	$N = 32$ (40%)

The composite score was also found to be a convenient way for exploring the effects respectively of degree of physical impairment and of environmental circumstances on 'outcomes'. The latter were defined in terms of a child's intellectual, educational, and emotional functioning.

'Outcomes' in relation to environmental circumstances and degree of physical handicap. It is, of course, well known that from the earliest age both the environment and any handicap play a vital formative role in the development of a child's potential, be this intellectual, emotional or educational. Previous research suggests that the extent to which a handicapped child is able to fulfil his potential is as much, if not more, affected by environmental conditions, especially parental attitudes, as it is by the actual degree of physical handicap (Pringle, 1964). Hence one would predict that in this group of thalidomide children, the most favourable environment would lead to the most satisfactory all-round functioning. To test this hypothesis, the children's intellectual functioning, educational achievement and emotional/social adjustment were examined, irrespective of their degree of physical handicap (Table 13 and detailed results for each child in Appendix D).

Table 13 'Outcomes' in relation to environmental circumstances

Environ. rating	No. of children	Intellect. functioning	Educat. achievt.	Emotion. adjustmt.	Total of mean scores
1 = most favourable	30	2·3*	2·2	1·4	5·9
2	27	3·2	3·0	2·3	8·5
3	13	3·2	3·2	3·2	9·6
4	5	4·0	4·4	3·8	12·2
5 = least favourable	5	3·8	4·8	3·2	11·8

* Average or mean rating for each sub-group.

As predicted, the children whose environmental circumstances are the most favourable, have consistently lower, i.e. more satisfactory, average scores than those from the least favourable backgrounds. This trend is most marked and consistent in relation to educational achievement. It is worth mentioning that among the group whose all-round functioning is most satisfactory, a sizeable proportion have quite a severe degree of handicap (three cases have a rating of 5 and four a rating of 4; see Appendix F, p. 82).

Secondly, the position was reversed, and 'outcomes' were examined in relation to the degree of physical handicap irrespective of environmental circumstances. The least handicapped child would, of course, be expected to reach a more satisfactory level of intellectual, educational and emotional functioning if only because physical and mental functioning are so closely and inextricably interwoven right from the start. However, one would predict this relation to be no more marked than that found with regard to environmental factors.

The same trend was found to operate here as did in relation to environmental conditions: the less severe the handicap, the lower, i.e. the more satisfactory, the average scores for intellectual, educational and emotional functioning (Table 14 and Appendix D). However, this

Table 14 'Outcomes' in relation to degree of physical handicap

Physical handicap rating	No. of children	Intellect. functioning	Educat. achievt.	Emotion. adjustmt.	Total of mean scores
1 = slight	18	2·4*	2·5	1·9	6·8
2	16	2·8	2·3	1·8	6·9
3	22	3·1	3·3	2·7	9·1
4	11	3·0	3·5	1·7	8·2
5 = v. severe	13	3·5	3·6	3·1	10·2

* Average or mean rating for each sub-group.

trend is both less marked and less consistent than it was in relation to environmental conditions. In general, then, the less severe the handicap and the more favourable the environmental conditions, the more likely that a thalidomide child will realise his potential capacities for growth and development.

7. Present schooling in relation to educational achievement

All the children were at school at the time of the study except three; two of these were just due to start and the third had been placed in a subnormality hospital. About half the group had had some preschool experience in nursery classes, nursery schools, preschool play groups or private kindergartens. In some cases this had been for a matter of weeks only, while in the case of those children who had attended the nursery, which was established by Glasgow Corporation specifically for thalidomide children at Parkhouse School for the partially hearing, it amounted to almost two years. Additionally, many had been admitted to their special school before they had reached the statutory age.

It must be regarded as highly satisfactory that such a sizeable proportion of children had been given the opportunity of some preschool experience. Both the parents and the authorities concerned seem to have been aware of how helpful this would be for later development and to have acted accordingly.

Before considering the children's present educational placement a comment on the Scottish school system might clarify what follows. The tradition of public (in the sense of State) education is so widely accepted by all social classes that there are comparatively few private or Church schools of any denominations; however, there exists in certain local authorities, especially in the cities, a fee-paying system, even for the primary age. Whatever the theoretical basis for selection, in practice there is fierce competition for places in these schools which are generally regarded as both academically and socially superior. They are rather on a par with the endowed or grant-aided day schools also existing in these cities, though Corporation school fees are rather lower than those of endowed schools. Such schools also operate a selection system based, partly at least, on intellectual ability. In fact, both types of schools select (or attempt to) an academic elite at 5 rather than at 12 years of age. Both of these are grouped together as fee-paying in our classification of types of school (Table 15).

Table 15 Type of school attended

School	Boys	Girls	Both	% of whole group
Primary (State) school (including 3 over-age girls)	20	23	43	54
Fee-paying of some kind	4	4	8	10
Special Schools				
for the physically handicapped	11	8	19	24
for the deaf	1	5	6	8
for the partially hearing	—	3	3	3
Mental subnormality hospital (deaf child)	1	—	1	1

The majority of the children, some 64 per cent, were being educated in ordinary schools; of the 35 per cent in special schools, twice as many went to schools for the physically handicapped as did to schools catering for children with impaired hearing. One child, judged to be unsuitable for education, was placed in a hospital (Table 15). If the 'authentic' thalidomide children only are considered, then some 53 per cent are attending ordinary and the remainder special schools. The vast majority – all but 10 per cent – are at day schools and four pupils are weekly boarders at a special school for the deaf. In cases of deafness, this handicap takes precedence over any limb deficiencies in deciding the appropriate schooling.

In terms of tested intelligence, the children at fee-paying schools are brightest and those in special schools dullest; while the pupils attending State primary schools are, as a group, markedly more able than those in special schools of one kind or another. There are probably several, possibly overlapping reasons to account for this situation.

To begin with, fee-paying schools operate a selection system based mainly on intellectual ability; an I.Q. of 115 is generally the minimum acceptable. From the outset, therefore, average and dull children are excluded. Only one of the severely handicapped group happened to have an I.Q. in this upper range of ability. The child in question lived in an area where such selective schools do not exist but where the local primary school was prepared to do everything possible to meet her special needs. The parents seem to be entirely satisfied with the education she is receiving and the progress she is making.

On the other hand, two of the children at fee-paying schools are already finding the pressure too great, showing signs of stress and maladjustment, even though both are only moderately disabled (short arms) and of good average ability. Of course, when assessing likely causes of emotional difficulties, home circumstances must be taken into account. In both these cases, parental expectations are high, thus acting in turn as an incentive and as a source of anxiety to all concerned. Neither child's parents have had an academic education or professional training of any kind. In both cases the mother is rather a perfectionist and very determined that her child should reach a high academic achievement. The fathers concur though in a more passive manner.

A further limiting factor regarding attendance at a fee-paying school lies in the fact that the parents have to be able to afford the fees even though the amount is fairly modest. Again, this favours the better off and hence probably more intelligent or educated home.

Turning now to the question why pupils attending special schools were found to be less intellectually able than those going to ordinary schools, it is necessary to consider the criteria which determine admission to a special school. Broadly speaking these are whether a child can cope – physically, educationally and emotionally – with the work and life of an ordinary school; or, conversely, whether the school feels it can provide adequately for his physical, educational and emotional needs. Clearly those whose physical handicap is most severe present the greatest challenge to the staff of an ordinary school; hence they are more likely to be recommended for transfer to a special school; and in general the more severely handicapped, it will be recalled, were also found to be less able.

Secondly, being more severely handicapped, they are likely to miss school more often because of treatment needs; this, together with their more limited intellectual ability, is likely to have an adverse effect on their scholastic progress. Thirdly, being less able, they probably find it much more difficult to compensate, i.e. to 'find ways round', so as to overcome their disability and hence they grow more backward educationally. Fourthly, our evidence suggests that the more severe the handicap, the greater the probability of some emotional difficulties – a further reason likely to lead to a child being recommended for special schooling. In some cases, too, unfavourable home circumstances play a part in such a recommendation.

In the light of all these considerations one would expect pupils in special schools to be not only intellectually less able but also educationally more backward than their counterparts in ordinary primary schools. Once in a special school, further unfavourable factors are likely to operate: usually the day is shorter which reduces time for learning and also the more handicapped children are likely to need more time off for treatments of various kinds. For quite a few, the rather lengthy journey to school may be tiring; some of the larger prostheses are heavy and unwieldy, and may thus be particularly trying and exhausting for young children. Next, because there are more intellectually dull children in special schools, the standard of expectation may well be lower; this in turn, could lead to lowered performance, even in the abler child.

4. Findings for Various Sub-groups

The primary aim of the survey was to assess the educational problems arising from the special needs and circumstances of thalidomide children. As the investigation progressed it became clear that in addition to problems common to the whole group, there was a clustering of difficulties, sometimes exclusive, sometimes overlapping, associated with specific sub-groups. Some of the groups are considered in their entirety, for example, all the institutionalised children and all those suffering from some degree of auditory impairment; while in respect of other groups only the most extreme cases are examined, such as the most intelligent children or the most emotionally disturbed. Some children appear in more than one sub-group; for example, a highly intelligent child may be attending a fee-paying school.

Ten groups will be considered; the first five contain the most extreme cases while the next five groups consist of all the children in the particular category. Each group will be considered from the point of view of intelligence, adjustment, home background and schooling.

Extreme cases

1. Children with minimal defects (though 'authentic' thalidomide): $N = 15$.
2. The most severely limb deficient: $N = 16$.
3. Highly intelligent children: $N = 6$.
4. Very dull children: $N = 7$.
5. The most maladjusted children: $N = 9$.

All children

6. Children with impaired hearing (deaf and partially hearing): $N = 20$.
7. Pupils in special schools for the physically handicapped: $N = 19$.
8. 'Accelerated' fee-paying pupils: $N = 8$.
9. Non-thalidomide children, including 'over-age' children: $N = 11$.
10. Rejected, institutionalised children: $N = 5$.

1. Children with minimal defects

Of the genuine thalidomide cases, some fifteen (or 25 per cent) were only mildly damaged.

Intelligence. Three very able (I.Q.s 130+); four above average; seven average; one dull.

Adjustment. Only a few were even mildly unsettled; one of these had suffered such prolonged hospital treatment and so much publicity, that normal adjustment could hardly be expected. The three very able children were markedly stable and well-adjusted.

Home background. Generally favourable; three children were rather over-protected by their mothers; one father was in prison and there was one child whose parents had been divorced. Overall, it looks as if the parents felt able to cope without additional help since none of those with the least damaged children had made contact with the Lady Hoare Fund.

Schooling. All the children are attending ordinary schools, five of them as fee-paying pupils. They would seem to be appropriately placed and the brightest children in particular are doing extremely well. In no case does the defect seem to have handicapped the child and there are no indications, at least at present, that special provision needs to be planned for later schooling or for vocational training. It should prove possible for at least seven of the children to go on to some form of higher education.

2. The most severely limb-deficient

All of these sixteen children are 'genuine' thalidomide cases. The most grossly damaged among them are five children who are virtually without any usable limb.

Intelligence. Majority of average ability; one boy has specific visuo-spatial ability; one able child; one dull.

Adjustment. A remarkable degree of stability is shown by this group of most severely damaged children. Very few symptoms of emotional disturbance are reported by either their parents or teachers; four children appear to be mildly maladjusted. Two other children, both of whom are rejected and institutionalised, are also rather insecure and anxious.

Home background. This group comes from the most diverse backgrounds. Four children have remarkably stable, supportive, sensible families whose concern is for the child's best interest, who are loving but non-indulgent; all the four children are themselves exceptionally well-adjusted. It is probably no accident that all have younger siblings–their parents have felt able to cope not only with a very severely handicapped child but with extending their families further.

Five other children have a reasonably favourable background and are also well-adjusted or only very mildly unsettled themselves.

At the other extreme three children are institutionalised–rejected by mothers who are, or have been, psychiatrically disabled. In three more cases the child is the object of the most overt maternal aggressiveness and financial compensation looms large in the minds of all three. One father is chronically disabled too. The parents of two children are divorced and there is open marital disharmony in at least another four cases.

Every one of these children was already known to the Lady Hoare Fund. Whether the parents could cope or not, additional help was both very necessary and much welcomed.

Schooling. Thirteen children are attending special schools for the physically handicapped, three of which are residential. The other three are in ordinary primary schools and are doing well educationally, one girl being an exceptionally good reader. On the other hand, the achievement of the special school pupils is less satisfactory: nine out of thirteen are backward in both English and arithmetic. Most of these children will require special educational provision throughout their school days, followed by sheltered conditions for further training and employment.

3. Highly intelligent children

There are six able or very able children (I.Q. 120 and above) among the 'authentic' thalidomide cases. None is severely damaged physically, but four have short arms with twisted hands; one has a short leg and blind eye; and one has a short left arm.

Intelligence. Three very able (I.Q. 130+); three able (I.Q. 120+).

Adjustment. Four children are regarded by their teachers as stable and two as mildly disturbed; both of these have experienced considerable disruptions in their school career involving changes of residence as well as schools.

Home background. All come from good homes with healthy, sensible, supportive but non-indulgent parents. In one case the father is absent but there is support from the extended family. Except for one boy who is an only child, there are other siblings. None of the parents expressed any wish for preferential treatment.

Schooling. Each of the six children seems to be a well-integrated, accepted member of his school community. They are making good progress educationally, being one or two years ahead of their age group in reading and arithmetic achievements. Thus the present educational provision can be regarded as satisfactory. The children are doing well and no one expressed a need or desire for change of any kind. The parents hope that the children will continue to be given the opportunity to remain in ordinary schools. There is no reason to suppose that they will not be able to do so at the secondary and, indeed, the tertiary stage of more advanced education, possibly to university level. Later on limb defects may become a handicap for laboratory or other technical skills, but given adequate guidance, it should be possible to channel their talents into areas in which they can successfully compete.

Should it be thought desirable at a later stage to provide special educational opportunities for these able children, as a group this would have to be done on a national basis which inevitably means residential facilities. If a similar proportion of highly intelligent thalidomide children were found to exist among the English and Welsh group, the likely total number in the whole of the United Kingdom would be in the region of fifty to sixty cases.

Alternatively, if an accelerated, grammar school type of education were provided for all types of physically handicapped children of high intelligence, then there would be enough pupils to warrant day provision in urban centres of population. However, none of the parents in our study expressed a wish for any special provision; on the contrary, they want their children to remain in the 'normal' stream of education.

4. Very dull children

Excluding those with impaired hearing, whose potential was difficult to assess, there were about as many very dull as very able children. Only two of the seven cases were 'authentically' thalidomide.

Intelligence. Seven children with an I.Q. below 80.

Adjustment. Three are regarded by their teachers as seriously maladjusted; three are judged to be moderately disturbed; one is thought to be only mildly unsettled.

Home background. In marked contrast to the previous group, this is strikingly unfavourable. One father has a prison record; another is quite indifferent towards his child; a third father is overtly rejecting the child and seeking residential accommodation; two children are both rejected and institutionalised; and a sixth lives almost permanently with grandparents because of parental inadequacy. Two of the mothers are receiving psychiatric treatment. Three children come from large families (four or more children).

Schooling. Four children are at ordinary primary schools and three in special schools for the physically handicapped. But for the physical defects, they would be more appropriately placed in classes or schools for the educationally subnormal. Educational achievements are very low, especially among those at special schools. The children in ordinary schools show some signs of better ability such as a good spoken vocabulary or some reading attainment. For these multiply disadvantaged children, thalidomide limb deficiencies do appear to constitute a real handicap. Their limited learning potential and unstimulating, disturbed home background combine to militate against their chance of coping with and overcoming their physical disabilities. It is recommended that those attending ordinary schools would benefit from being transferred to special schools where the multiplicity of their handicaps could be more appropriately catered for. Eventually this group will require sheltered occupational conditions. If they remain in their present schools, it is highly likely that there will be further deterioration both in attainments and adjustment.

5. The most maladjusted children

This group of nine children contains four profoundly deaf children; the other five have moderately serious physical handicaps.

Intelligence. One very able (a deaf child); three average ability; five dull or very dull.

Adjustment. All are considered by their teachers to be seriously maladjusted.

Home background. This is atypical or unfavourable in every case. None of the fathers is playing a positive role, being either dead, absent, indifferent or still denying the reality of the child's disability. The two least disturbed children have accepting mothers; in the other cases, they are comparatively dull or helpless, or have had psychiatric treatment.

Seven of the homes suffer from poverty and low cultural standards.

Clearly it cannot be said that thalidomide is responsible for the children's severe maladjustment. Rather it is the combined effects of a poor social and psychological background combined with the physical disabilities caused by the drug which account for the total handicap.

Schooling. The educational placement of four children needs to be given urgent consideration: the first is attending an 'accelerated' primary school for bright children; being of only average intelligence she is finding the educational pressure too much and the situation is made worse by excessive family ambition. Sights will need to be set at a lower, more realistic level and much counselling will be required if parental acceptance of the child's handicaps and real needs is to be achieved.

Secondly, two educationally subnormal children, who are at present in ordinary schools might be more appropriately placed in special schools.

Thirdly, a deaf, very dull child attending a special school for the deaf, seems emotionally highly vulnerable because of sensory and emotional deprivation. He might be better placed in a school or class for the educationally subnormal, or failing that, in a mental subnormality hospital.

6. Children with impaired hearing

It is this group of twenty children which probably presents the most serious and largely unacknowledged, problem in the whole thalidomide disaster. They constitute a third of the 'authentic' cases. Eight of them are virtually earless and hence profoundly deaf; two have one ear only; three have such severe auditory impairment or have such deformed ears, that they require special schooling for the partially hearing; and a further seven have some hearing loss in addition to other defects.

Not only is this group numerically the largest single one, but auditory impairment has the most detrimental effects on language development, socialisation and communication, and on the growth of intellectual ability itself. Thus the severely deaf child may have little if any comprehensible speech, his intellectual potential may be seriously underdeveloped or underestimated, he presents severe educational problems and is psychologically very vulnerable. Yet this effect of thalidomide has received little public acknowledgement or sympathy compared with that accorded to limb deficiencies.

To make matters even more difficult for this group, all but three of these children suffer from additional defects. Most of the earless have some visual defect, ranging from one blind eye to squints and forward vision only; and there is also a high incidence of facial paralysis which not only affects speech but also detracts further from the children's appearance. Even then the catalogue of damage is not ended: two of the profoundly deaf have no thumbs, another partially hearing child has very short arms and the group is further afflicted by defects of heart, kidney, ankles, palate and sex organs.

Intelligence. Could not be reliably assessed.

Adjustment. Five of the profoundly deaf children are severely maladjusted, showing a great variety of symptoms. A further two are markedly disturbed emotionally. The three partially hearing children all show signs of moderate maladjustment, according to their teachers. Of the two children who each lack one ear, one is thoroughly stable but the other, reported to be moderately disturbed by her present teacher, has, in fact, already had psychiatric treatment. She is the only child too, who to our knowledge, has been referred for treatment on her own account for manifest behaviour disorders. The remaining children who are mildly deaf or suspected of suffering some hearing loss, run the whole gamut from one boy who is reported to be entirely stable to three moderately and two considerably disturbed children on to one who is said to be very severely maladjusted. He is, however, a child who has multiple defects and disadvantages besides his hearing defect.

Home background. Of the profoundly deaf children only two have reasonably favourable backgrounds, though in both cases the parents are supportive in a weak and indulgent manner rather than stimulating. In two cases emotional disturbance is very apparent in both mothers and, by inference, in the fathers too. In two further cases the fathers have died and both widows are left with very large families (six and ten children respectively) to care for. One boy, mentioned already, is the child of a very young, deserting and now divorced mother; the paternal relatives care about his welfare but are unable to cope with his mental and physical disabilities and have had to place him in a residential institution. The parents of another child are permanently resident abroad and though she, too, has caring relatives, in her case exceptionally devoted grandmothers, the family structure is inevitably atypical, in that it lacks a permanent male figure.

The three children at special schools for the partially hearing all have more or less normal family backgrounds, with concerned, supportive parents.

Of the other children who have minor or only suspected hearing defects, roughly half have normal backgrounds; the other half suffer from a wide range of disadvantages, from excessive paternal or maternal indulgence to parental indifference, and from having a step-parent to being rejected and institutionalised.

Schooling. Of the twenty children, nine are appropriately placed in special schools for the deaf or partially hearing and three are in special schools for the physically handicapped. Seven are in ordinary schools and one in a mental subnormality hospital.

At present, an alternative placement would seem advisable for three of the children: one is struggling in an ordinary school because the area lacks specialist provision for the deaf, one pupil in a special school is of such limited ability and so disturbed psychologically that she might receive more appropriate care in a school for the educationally subnormal or in a hospital environment; and one, a pupil at a school for the physically handicapped, is making such inadequate progress that he might well benefit from transfer to a unit or school for those with partial hearing.

7. Pupils in special schools for the physically handicapped

The majority (fifteen of the nineteen children) are attending day schools and four are in residential schools. Of this latter group three live in residential homes because of parental rejection (they are included also in group 10).

Intelligence. Two good average; nine average; five low average; three dull.

Adjustment. Two children are severely and one boy is markedly maladjusted. The three institutionalised children are moderately disturbed; a further six cases are mildly disturbed; and seven children are reported to be reasonably adjusted.

Home background. Four children have a most favourable family background where there is acceptance, love and support; in nine cases there is a reasonably happy, stable and accepting home. Of the remaining six children, one has a step-father whom his mother married after a divorce, one has an indifferent father and a third child's father is physically disabled and an inadequate personality; three children have been rejected by their parents and live in residential care (they are described in group 10).

Schooling. In a number of instances, schools for the physically handicapped have premises adjoining a school for the mentally handicapped; this means that their respective pupils travel on the same bus. Where there are parental objections to special school placement, this aspect tends to be the focus of criticism: 'it's the stigma'; 'people say he goes to the "dafties" school'. The fact that transport arrangements substantially reduce the length of the actual school day also gives concern since it curtails the amount of education received by the children.

How do these special school children compare with their counterparts who attend ordinary schools? All have moderate to very severe physical disabilities, whereas this is the case for half of the pupils in ordinary schools, the others being only mildly disabled; nevertheless, one severely disabled girl (virtually limbless) and two armless children manage quite well to hold their own in ordinary schools (Table 16).

Table 16 Degree of handicap in relation to type of school

Handicapped	Ordinary school	School for the physically handicapped
1. Minimal	4	—
2. Slight	11	—
3. Moderate	14	5
4. Severe	2	9
5. Very severe	1	4
	$N = 32$	$N = 18$

What seems to determine placement is partly local facilities and partly a combination of home circumstances and intellectual potential. A few children of average ability and with favourable, supportive home backgrounds, are in some parts of the country sent to special schools whereas their counterparts in other areas are accepted and made welcome in ordinary schools. In parental eyes, at least, this is felt to be 'unjust' because it is thought that children in ordinary schools are given better opportunities to reach higher standards of achievement. Most parents want their children to live at home and to be accepted as well as integrated in their local community; it is felt that if they were sent to a boarding school for the thalidomide or for physically handicapped children, they would become even more 'special' than they are already.

The degree of educational backwardness found among this group attending special schools for the physically handicapped was rather high: only three are working at about their own age level; five children are described by their teachers as good and nine as poor readers; and in arithmetic, only two are classed as good and ten as poor achievers. Thus about seven or eight children are under-achieving in their school work; this is a considerable proportion considering that most are of about average ability. However, they are reasonably well adjusted emotionally while the comparable group in ordinary schools show a greater or lesser degree of emotional difficulties.

This allows of two diametrically opposed arguments: on the one hand, one might suppose that because they are stable, no harm is likely to come from greater educational expectation and an increased pace; on the other hand, it might be thought that increased pressure could result in increased tension which may well lead to emotional difficulties. However, in view of the fact that educational retardation tends to be cumulative and inevitably also lessens the chances of transfer to an ordinary school, it would be worthwhile to explore the effects of trying to bring their school work nearer to the normal level for their age. Clearly this must be done with care and with due regard to the individual circumstances of each pupil.

8. 'Accelerated' fee-paying pupils

Of the eight children, six are definitely in the thalidomide group and two are doubtful cases; the latter have only slight defects. To be accepted in fee-paying primary schools, children are expected to be of above average ability and this is the case for all but two of the pupils.

Intelligence. One very able (I.Q. 130+); three able (I.Q 120+); two good average.

Adjustment. The two girls who are of average ability only, are reported to be respectively unsettled and maladjusted; one able boy is also said to be 'seriously unsettled'. The others are coping well.

Home background. The economic circumstances of all the homes in this group are comfortable and family relationships are, in general, good and supporting. In the case of all three emotionally unsettled children, however, there is intense parental pressure towards academic achievements and high hopes for eventual success in a profession.

Schooling. One girl of average intelligence is considered backward and maladjusted by her school. An alternative placement would be advisable since in an educationally less demanding environment her attainment would be quite satisfactory for her age. Less taxing expectations might well have a beneficial effect on her emotional adjustment. The second girl seems able to cope educationally, though her intelligence is borderline for her particular school. Because of her emotional difficulties she needs continuing and careful observation. If her behaviour deteriorates, a similar transfer may be of benefit in her case. Overall, it seems that physical disabilities, whatever their origin, need not be an obstacle to educational progress in a highly competitive educational setting.

9. Non-thalidomide children, including 'over age' children

Though their names appeared on the Scottish Education Department's list, the children were eventually found not to be thalidomide cases. Because their handicaps were very similar and, but for one exception, rather mild, they have been included in the study.

Intelligence. Four very able; seven average.

Adjustment. Good except for one boy. He is the brightest of the group and his physical defect is a very minor one. However, his parents are making such strenuous efforts to ignore or even deny its presence that the boy is being subjected to an unrealistically high expectation to reach absolute normality.

Home background. This is generally favourable (both socially and economically) except for one older girl who comes from a rather limited rural background. Without exception, the families are wholeheartedly accepting, and concerned for the children – in one case to a misguided degree of over-anxiety.

Schooling. Except for one grossly handicapped boy, all are in ordinary schools. There they are doing well and are accepted by their classmates. Hence they can be regarded as satisfactorily placed. The child who is attending a special school is very backward educationally but considering how much schooling he has missed, particularly during the initial stages, his achievements are really very creditable.

10. Rejected, institutionalised children

Of the five children living in institutions, all are affected by adverse family backgrounds in addition to their physical disabilities.

Intelligence. Two average ability; two very dull; one mentally subnormal.

Adjustment. One child is deeply disturbed, the other four are emotionally disturbed to various degrees.

Home background. Circumstances vary so much that no generalised picture is possible. One deaf, earless boy is in a hospital for subnormal children. His parents are divorced and have rejected him, but the paternal grandmother has concern for him. Unless a specialist investigation can elicit greater signs of educable capacity, he is suitably placed.

The second and third, a boy and a girl, are virtually limbless and are rejected by their psychiatrically disabled mothers. There is little doubt that they are appropriately placed in a residential home which has its own school for the physically handicapped.

The fourth child lives in a local authority Children's Home. He has short arms and is blind in one eye. He comes from a large tinker family which has rejected him.

The fifth comes from a broken home, the father having deserted and remarried. After initial difficulties the mother now manages to take the child home for holidays but during term time she lives in a residential home. The girl too is severely disabled physically.

Schooling. The tinker boy attends an ordinary school in the neighbourhood of the residential home. At present his attainments are minimal and unless he begins to improve, the question of transfer to a special school for the educationally subnormal will need to be considered. Two children who are of at least average intelligence, and one who is rather dull, are attending residential schools attached to their Homes for the physically handicapped. Though some severely handicapped but intelligent children do manage to hold their own in ordinary schools, there is less hope that any of these three children could do so since they are already educationally backward and emotionally unsettled. However, one, the brightest boy, might benefit from transfer to a residential Home for the physically handicapped which has a school of its own with standards geared to the average and above, rather than average and below.

5. Six Case Studies

To help bring to life the more generalised findings for the whole group of children and the special sub-groups, six case studies are presented in some detail, together with some examples of drawings and handwriting. Descriptions but with fictitious names are given of:

1. Fiona – who is severely disabled but managing well in an ordinary school;
2. Tommy – an under-achieving child of average intelligence who is moderately disabled;
3. Pat – a mildly disabled, over-protected boy who is psychologically vulnerable;
4. Gerry – a legless boy who is emotionally disturbed and educationally backward;
5. Jane – who is also legless but coping extremely well;
6. Cathy – an earless, deaf child.

These case studies illustrate that emotional adjustment and educational progress depend as much, if not more, on parental love and acceptance as on the type or severity of the physical disability.

1. Fiona – who is severely disabled but managing well in an ordinary school

An alert-looking little girl approaching 7 years, who has no arms and whose hips are so dislocated that she cannot walk. At present she does everything with her feet but if an operation to straighten her legs enabled her to walk, she might well lose some of her present dexterity. She would then have to learn to use artificial arms.

On all the tests Fiona shows superior ability and is making very efficient use of her capacities. Her educational attainments are a year, and in some respects two years, ahead of her chronological age. Indeed, her achievements are above what one would expect of her measured intelligence and since there is no evidence of excessive pressure at home

7 yr level T-M
Copying a diamond

9 yr level T-M
Reproduced from memory

Fiona. Aged 6 yrs 9 mths   *done entirely with her feet*

or at school, this suggests even greater endowment than her test scores indicate. She is particularly well advanced in reading and in verbal reasoning; in arithmetic she is nearer the average for her age. Her grasp of spatial relationships and her ability to produce accurate diagrams are remarkable considering her physical limitations; her free drawing is less controlled but full of energy and colour, though not perhaps highly creative. Her approach to all situations is sensible and practical.

Fiona is a very stable and well-adjusted child according to all reports and all the present evidence. She is the middle one in a family of three with very sensible, supportive parents. They are living in a rural area and Fiona attends the local village school. Some adaptations of desks and toilet arrangements were necessary but otherwise she has been no trouble to her teachers and is fully accepted as an ordinary pupil.

All her early history confirms the impression of a bright child of good personality and with a good environment who responds to the challenge of her disabilities with her full potential. Her mother reports that though Fiona had to spend her first eighteen months in plaster from knees to shoulders she refused a bottle in favour of a cup at 5 months old, began to speak at 8 months and to use her feet for all sorts of activities the moment the plaster was removed. Half of her first five years was spent in hospital where she fretted badly for company and probably also for the stimulation denied her in the rather strict ward conditions. Her mother describes her as 'a bit shy and she won't talk back though she's fine with children, even showing off at times'.

Clearly her present schooling is entirely appropriate. In normal circumstances she would undoubtedly be capable of profiting from advanced education; considering her present level of achievement the prognosis would seem to be equally and wholly favourable despite the severity of her physical handicaps. Her intelligence and personality assets are such that no serious difficulty need be anticipated if she continues to be supplied with any artificial, manipulative or motor aids which may become available. Fiona's physical defect may even mask some of her full potential, but, very severe though it is, she can be said to be surmounting it. She is an excellent example of the physically severely disabled child who, with a completely accepting, loving, sensible home and with full co-operation from education authorities and teachers, can not only cope but do remarkably well in an ordinary school.

2. Tommy – an under-achieving child of average intelligence who is moderately disabled

A tall, handsome, active 7-year-old with a mop of curly black hair. Tommy has very short arms with inward twisted hands at about elbow level and no thumbs. He is not as bright as Fiona but his intelligence on most of the formal measures is consistently average and he works tidily and conscientiously. He went to Glasgow Corporation's specially established nursery school for thalidomide children for over a year, and then was sent on to a special school for physically handicapped children, where he is said to be doing poorly at classwork. On the tests used he was quite unable to read and his vocabulary was simple and limited for his age; he had some grasp of arithmetic but his manual dexterity was poor and erratic.

Considering his potential Tommy is thus quite seriously retarded. This is more likely to be attributable to environmental circumstances than to the physical defect, which is not as disastrously handicapping as some. His level of maturity is below average and he is not making the

Draw a man

T-M 5 yr level *Copying square*

T-M 7 yr level *Copying diamond*

12 3 4 5 6 7 8 9 10 11 12

(I am six)

Tommy. Aged 6 yrs 2 mths

fullest use of his ability in his present school. Whether he could catch up enough to hold his own in an ordinary school is doubtful and his expressed ambition to become a teacher is most unlikely to be realised.

More seriously disturbing than his comparative scholastic retardation, however, is the report of maladjusted behaviour at school. Tommy is said to be 'jumpy and excitable', extremely restless and very anxious about adult interest and affection and, though physically well cared for, has a disturbed home background. At birth he was rejected by his mother and looked after by other relatives for a time. Now his parents do care about him but he is spoilt, indulged and over-protected by them and other relatives. In his home he has experienced the effects of unemployment, psychiatric illness, alcoholism and an intermittently broken home life. He has also lost a lot of schooling (but not on account of treatment for thalidomide damage), still has toilet difficulties and suffers from a speech defect.

Tommy is one of the children affected by environmental handicaps of a kind which might beset any child. Educationally he requires special provision, primarily for social reasons. In another area, or with a different home background, he might be doing well in an ordinary school. As it is, he seems all set to become increasingly underprivileged; though the family are not asking for special provision and might not welcome it, this looks the kind of situation where in the child's best long-term interests residential schooling might be considered.

3. Pat – a mildly disabled, over-protected boy who is psychologically vulnerable

Pat is the second child of rather older parents who live in comfortable working class circumstances in a small industrial town. He looks for all the world like any other well-developed, well-cared-for 7 year old. During the interview, however, he remained silent and stood apart until his mother took off his coat and added her encouragement to the invitation to sit down to have a look at books and toys ready on a table for him. He remained passive while obviously listening hard; he answered politely, but in a very flat voice; and he sat quite expressionless when reference was made to his handicap, which is comparatively speaking very slight – his left arm ends in a rounded stump at wrist level. His mother did all the talking, though she looked to father for agreement. It soon became clear that there was some strain in the family's efforts to avoid words such as 'handicap', 'defect', 'difficulty' or 'difference'; to underline this attitude, Pat is and has been regarded and treated as completely normal.

Both parents frankly admit that the child's defect made them very unhappy and they still feel they can never forget or get over it; however, this was only expressed when Pat was out of earshot. He was relatively quick at reaching physical milestones but talked late and was never a good eater or sleeper. The mother worried, feeling she had to shield him all the time; she still cannot accept her own sister's urging to allow Pat to go to the baths and to play football with other children, or to permit him to go on his own to the school playground.

During the interview Pat was found to be obsessionally tidy and one of the few pieces of information he volunteered was that he didn't like painting lessons because you 'got in a mess'. At school he is no trouble at all, though his teacher regards his lack of naughtiness as not altogether a virtue and comments on his solitariness and tendency to be an onlooker rather than a participant. He is an intelligent child, in the top section of his class at an ordinary school, doing well but not brilliantly in all subjects. Both parents are emphatic that education 'matters' and that he must get as much as possible; to enable him to do so they send him to a school with a good academic reputation. Pat, then, seems

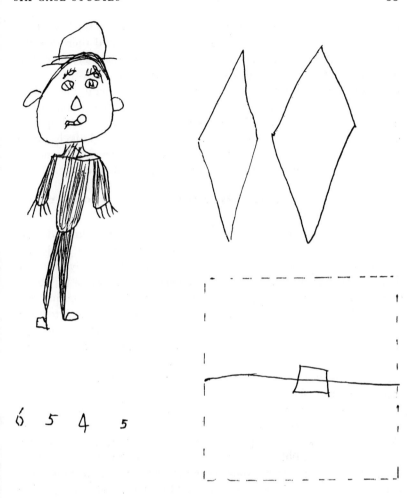

Pat. Aged 6 yrs 8 mths

destined for a straightforward, carefully controlled career as a 'good' pupil, who will successfully pass examinations and take certificates and diplomas until he emerges as a well-qualified white-collar or professional worker.

Neither Pat nor his family would see any need for help or for any change in the well-ordered, self-sufficient lives they lead themselves and foresee for him. But psychologically he is a vulnerable child, not overtly handicapped by his relatively minor deformity but already damaged to some extent by over-protectiveness and the dependency, isolation and withdrawal which have resulted from it. Pat is seriously 'unsettled' according to the Bristol Social Adjustment Guide and there is some suspicion that, though his school attainments are satisfactory, he may be underfunctioning a little already because of emotional constriction. He is in danger of becoming a crippled, inadequate personality, because of a misguided denial of a comparatively minor physical impairment; certain characteristics are already present which may develop into serious symptoms of emotional disturbance. Thus a relatively minor defect, which might have been relatively easily and cheerfully surmounted could, in this family context, become a definite handicap.

4. Gerry – a legless boy who is emotionally disturbed and educationally backward

Most of the Scottish thalidomide children have upper-limb defects. Gerry is one of the few who was born with rudimentary feet projecting awkwardly from the main trunk; in addition, he had slightly deformed hands with extra digits which were removed when he was a tiny baby, leaving him now virtually normal in this respect. When he was just over a year old, his feet were amputated at hip level and he was fitted with pylons; later he was given, and trained to walk with, artificial legs. As an infant he was in and out of hospital a great deal and though he went to a nursery school from the age of 3, he missed a lot of early primary education because of surgical operations on his stumps and physiotherapy requirements.

Gerry is the youngest in a large family and the older siblings complain about his being a nuisance; his father is not very interested in him either. While his mother is unhappy about the amount of time he is away from home for so much treatment, she would also like him to be able to do more of the things other children do, such as swimming, running fast, playing games in the street, and so on. Most stages of development are said to have been normal or even advanced. He was a bright and lively baby, and without behaviour difficulties as a young child, though the mother's frame of reference may not be reliable when she talks of 'average'. Now at the early school stage, he is becoming more 'difficult': he has temper tantrums 'like fits', he rages, cries and throws things; he is also said to have nightmares.

At the interview, the mother was anxious, worried and depressed; Gerry was silent and mulish, refusing to be separated from her even for a short time "cause I don't want her to go'. The test results indicate that Gerry is very dull and his troublesome behaviour seems fairly typical of the less well-endowed child, exacerbated by the frustrations of his leg-defect which prevent him from 'letting-off-steam' in physical activity as

T-M 7 yr level test
Copying diamond

Gerry. Aged 7 yrs 7 mths

his peers can do. His family background sounds troubled: he is partially rejected by those who would be his 'hero' figures and defended, if not over-protected, by his mother to whom he is clinging in a prolonged baby phase. In school, too, Gerry is one of the most seriously maladjusted children according to the Bristol Social Adjustment Guide; his symptoms take the form of restlessness and of great anxiety for the interest and affection of both children and adults combined with considerable hostility towards both.

Gerry is backward at all school subjects. He went first to an ordinary school but 'because of the stairs' was transferred to a special school for physically handicapped children. His mother feels he is doing even less well there because there are 'no books' and 'he has no books at home'. She considers that he should have as much education as possible and would like to help him at home if she only knew how, if the others would 'take a bit more time to do things with him' and if he was a bit more concerned to learn.

Alas, there is the rub. On all measures Gerry's I.Q. is between 70 and 80 and he is functioning more like a 5-year-old than a 7-year-old. He cannot read at all and shows not the slightest disposition to learn; he counts on his fingers but cannot add up; and he is inattentive and apathetic. All told, it is probable that, were it not for the physical defect, Gerry would have been transferred to a special class for slow-learning or educationally backward children. Apparently the possibility of impaired hearing has not been assessed though it may well be a vital contributory cause to his difficulties. The actual physical defect is of minor relevance to his educational progress. Understandably it adds to his psychological maladjustment but is by no means the only contributing factor.

For his own needs, Gerry is appropriately placed in a special school. Whether his presence hampers the learning pace and opportunities of some other, brighter children in the physically handicapped school, would be difficult to assess. Whether he would fit in better in a special class for the educationally backward is a matter for consideration in the light of his individual needs as well as local facilities. If his hearing were found to be impaired, this would also have to be taken into consideration. Because of his physical defect, his dullness, and the unfavourable environment, he needs extra care and support. In the long term he will probably require sheltered working conditions with very sympathetic, patient supervision as well as counselling, to enable him to develop what potential he possesses.

5. Jane, who like Gerry, is legless but is coping extremely well

A year older than Gerry, Jane too, has no legs. She is not a thalidomide child but she well might have been. Conversely Gerry might have been born with a congenital defect as Jane was. The differences between them are not attributable to the effects of the drug.

Because of a hereditary defect in the mother's family, Jane was born with club feet as well as hip and leg deformities which necessitated amputation above the knee. She too has a hand deformity with five fingers but no thumb on either hand. She too was fitted with pylons and then with artificial legs and has been much involved with hospital treatment, largely for training and enlargement of appliances.

Jane is now a solid, cheerful child approaching 9 years; emotionally very stable; doing well at an ordinary school and expected to proceed to secondary education with her classmates without anything more than special transport arrangements; she looks so normal that public transport is, in fact, dangerous for her as bus drivers are jerky and move off just too quickly for her safety. Being of average intelligence, her present

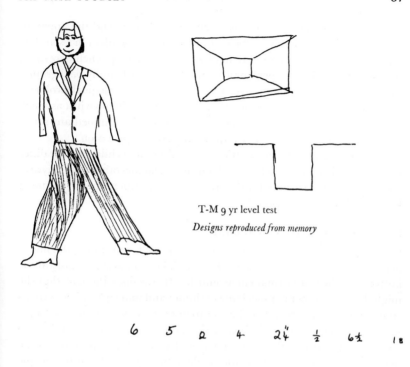

T-M 9 yr level test
Designs reproduced from memory

Jane. Aged 8 yrs 6 mths

ambition to become a typist or a hairdresser should be easily realised. Her teacher's comment on the Bristol Social Adjustment Guide admirably sums up our own assessment of the present situation.

'Jane is a perfectly adjusted, normal and delightful little girl who is conquering her serious physical handicaps courageously. She radiates happiness and contentment and our one fear is that when she becomes adolescent she may then realise the full extent of her disability and be less willing to accept it. In the meantime, she is treated by teachers and children alike as just another pupil and apart from exemption from part of the physical education lesson, she does not expect or receive any special concessions in school. Her written work is a model of neatness.'

Obviously this child's contentment reflects not only educational but environmental adjustment. For all that her mother declared that there were no early problems, there must have been a need for adjustments to be made. Even though the mother had experienced the effects of such a handicap in her own generation, and could foresee and anticipate some of the likely difficulties, the child had to learn to cope without legs, to accept the explanations she was given and to understand the apparent cruelty of others. She is being brought up to be independent in a sensible, loving home, with parents and an older sister who help when necessary, but do not spoil her. In personality, intelligence and family background Jane has many advantages over Gerry but the psychological problems she may yet have to face are no less serious and may involve just as much careful and continuous counselling. However, her immediate social and educational needs do not require any special provision.

Jane's case highlights how little some thalidomide children may differ from those with similar defects and how much factors other than physical disability are responsible for differences in adjustment and attainment between different individuals.

6. Cathy – an earless, deaf child

Cathy has a ridge of flesh on one side of her head, continuing the line of her jaw-bone, and on the other side a small knob of flesh, roughly at the bottom of where a normal ear would be. It was once thought that she might have the inner ear mechanisms intact and that surgical operations could open a channel and enable her to hear. However, several attempts to do so have failed and though she now wears a bone-conduction apparatus there is little hope that it will give her much help. So she lives in the silent world of the totally deaf. She can see that other people communicate in some way that she does not understand though she is gradually learning to interpret some of their meaning. She goes to a special school where there are ten or eleven other profoundly deaf children in her class.

Cathy, aged nearly $6\frac{1}{2}$ years, is a thalidomide victim. Whereas others affected by the drug were born without arms or legs, she and at least seven other Scottish children were born without ears. In addition she has some other defects; one arm is short and twisted; she is without thumbs; she has some minor internal deformities; there is a squint and some facial paralysis which deforms her mouth and makes articulation difficult. Any one of these is likely to handicap a child. Cathy is afflicted by multiple handicaps, the greatest of which is her profound deafness.

Furthermore she is the youngest of a very large family in poor circumstances and her father died when she was only a very small baby. Though her mother is rather overwhelmed by all her difficulties, she and the older brothers and sisters give Cathy a lot of attention and are very fond of her. The siblings closer in age are, in fact, said to be rather jealous of Cathy and there may later be less cheerfulness and kindness surrounding her, but so far she is a happy child and a 'trier'.

T-M 5 yr level test *Copying square*

T-M 7 yr level test *Copying diamond*

Cathy. 6 yrs 4 mths

Cathy was no particular bother as a baby except that she was never a good sleeper and is restless still. Already she has had quite a lot of hospital treatment and operations and there are more to come on her hands and ears. There is a general impression, conveyed by Mother and Granny, that no one fully understands how it all happened or why anything is proposed. 'They are awful abrupt and don't tell you much', but, somehow, out of what seems to them a lack of adequate communication Cathy is growing up, protected and sheltered at home, cared for by doctors, teachers and social workers who are doing their best to mitigate her difficulties.

First of all she went to a school for physically handicapped children but was soon transferred to a school for the deaf. Her teacher reports that Cathy is still very backward, restless, erratic and withdrawn. Though her behaviour is disturbed enough to add up to a picture of maladjustment, yet her teacher describes her sympathetically as 'a happy child who is determined to overcome her handicap, always ready to try'.

During the assessment interview it was very difficult to get through to her but she imitated actions as instructed and ordered her play quite purposefully, tidying away spontaneously, too. She is more accessible than some of the other deaf children but is not estimated to have more than dull to normal intelligence. Educationally she is still grossly retarded but specialist facilities are now available for her and she will have the full benefit of these. Her mother is worried about her inability to speak yet and about her hands but is pleased at her progress in the school for the deaf and very much wants her to stay there. The present provision is appropriate and no further educational difficulty is foreseen until the vocational stage is reached. At this point Cathy's hands may constitute an additional handicap and prevent her from pursuing some of the occupations open to other deaf pupils.

Whilst it is impossible to predict how she may develop and how many of her handicaps she may wholly or partially overcome, it is probable that sheltered working and living conditions may always have to be provided for her. There is some prospect that, given the continuance of a caring family background, Cathy's frustrations may diminish as she learns (by special methods) to communicate and that her present maladjustment will decrease as she makes educational progress. Though she has multiple defects and many environmental disadvantages, she seems to have considerable assets of personality and a remarkably supporting, warm psychological environment in which to grow up and develop.

6. Discussion of Main Findings

1. The sample and the assessment procedures

The two major sources used to identify children affected by the drug were the Lady Hoare Thalidomide Appeal and the Scottish Education Department. Though both keep up-to-date lists, in the event neither proved to be comprehensive. In fact, a few cases came to light only because a child was known to parents already taking part in the study. Hence identification was not as straightforward a process as might have been expected. A number of children were included whose handicap was thought not to be due to the drug. Of the eighty children eventually interviewed, three-quarters were judged to be 'authentic' thalidomide cases. Since in most instances the handicaps of the remainder were similar to and often indistinguishable from the others, they have for most purposes been treated as a single group.

There probably remain a number of unknown cases. Available evidence suggests that about 75 per cent of all children affected by the drug in Scotland have been included in this survey. No information is available on those who refused to co-operate and one can only speculate why they decided not to take part.

The main aim of the study was to explore the children's present as well as likely future educational needs. Therefore the tests chosen covered various aspects of intellectual development and scholastic achievement and they were supplemented by information obtained by interviewing both the child and one or both parents. An account of the child's behaviour and adjustment at school was provided by headteachers. It had been thought that full information was already available to the Appeal on each child's home background; so allowance was not made – either in terms of time or money – for gathering a detailed social history. Eventually it was found that this was rather sketchy and incomplete but by then it was too late to remedy the situation. In a number of cases this lack proved to be a considerable shortcoming.

Broadly speaking, the information collected fell into three parts: aspects of performance or behaviour which were measured or assessed; attitudes which were observed or inferred; and descriptive accounts which were given by those most closely concerned with the child in the everyday context of home and school.

2. The children

(a) Physical impairment

Overall this is a severely damaged group and many of the children have multiple handicaps. It is, however, fallacious to think that thalidomide has in all cases resulted in a readily recognisable, exclusive or specific type of defect or deformity. Limb deficiencies were the most frequent, affecting some two-thirds of the group. Next is impaired hearing which affected a third of the 'authentic' thalidomide cases; a further seven children were suspected of suffering from some auditory deficit. In addition, many children were afflicted by a number of other handicaps, ranging from visual and speech defects to facial paralysis and internal deformities.

Wide variation existed in the degree of handicap. This ranged from a missing thumb to the virtual absence of all limbs. In functional terms there were even greater differences, because the psychological impact of a particular impairment has very different effects on a particular child and his family. Hence one cannot readily predict from the type and degree of a defect the exact nature and severity of its disabling consequences. For example, a severely handicapped 7-year-old who has no arms and badly dislocated hips, is coping well in an ordinary school; she is intellectually able and emotionally well-adjusted and her parents are loving, supportive and sensible in their handling; she is completely accepted by them as well as by her school, and is meeting the challenge of her severe disabilities by making the fullest use of her potential. On the other hand, another 7-year-old who is relatively mildly disabled – being without a left hand and forearm – is withdrawn, solitary and emotionally over-dependent on his parents. Though he is doing quite well at school, where academic standards are high, his parents' inability to help him face and come to terms with his defect has made him psychologically very vulnerable.

While from the outset the spotlight has been on the limb deficiencies of thalidomide children, the extent and severity of auditory impairment seems to have remained largely unacknowledged. Yet this is as serious, and in quite a few cases a much more serious, disability because of its detrimental effects on every area of mental development: the ability to think and reason; to communicate and make relationships; to progress educationally – all of these are affected, and at worst, remain stunted. In addition, most of this group suffer from other defects too, as well as from the fact that of all handicaps, deafness receives the least public sympathy and understanding.

(b) Intellectual and language development

This ranged from the very dull to the very able, from the educationally subnormal to the potential university student. The group as a whole closely resembled the general child population: the majority were of average ability while a smaller proportion were intellectually able or very limited respectively (some 25 per cent in each case). Thus it can be concluded with confidence that the drug does not have a detrimental effect on the development of general learning potential.

(c) Educational attainments

It is now generally accepted that during the first few years of life a child learns more, and more rapidly, than during any comparable period subsequently. For any handicapped child the opportunities for learning during the preschool period are bound to be more limited: sensory and speech defects hinder in an all-pervasive way exploring, and thus getting to understand and master, the world around him; physical disabilities inevitably restrict – to a greater or lesser degree – the child's mobility and manipulative ability; to the extent that moving his limbs, crawling, walking, climbing, running, touching and handling are affected, to that extent experiences may either be curtailed or, at worst, be missed completely.

Since this early learning forms the basis or foundation for later progress at school, one would have expected a considerable proportion of thalidomide children to be educationally backward; all the more so since the need for frequent hospital visits as well as in-patient treatment is likely to interrupt regular school attendance. It is therefore very remarkable that about half the pupils had achieved an average reading level for their age: in fact, the number of good, average and poor readers was very similar to the proportions found in a normal sample of children. In arithmetic they did somewhat less well. Absence from school probably has a more deleterious effect on this subject because progress depends more directly on being taught the various steps and processes; whereas, once a child has made a beginning with reading, he can continue to a much greater extent by himself or without specific teaching.

Thus in this early stage of their educational career the group as a whole is making satisfactory progress. Such a level of scholastic achievement is a great credit not only to the children themselves but also to their parents and teachers. The fact that about half the group had been given the opportunity of some preschool experience has clearly been of tremendous value; as have been the guidance and stimulation given to a great many children in the Special Self-Care Unit of the Princess Margaret Rose Hospital, Edinburgh.

The majority attended ordinary primary schools, a small proportion going to 'accelerated' fee-paying ones, and about a third to day special schools of one kind or another. A very small number went to residential schools or lived in residential Homes.

(d) Emotional and social adjustment

Considering that all the children are disabled, and many of them to a very severe degree, the relatively low incidence of behaviour disturbances and difficulties is remarkable. In fact, the evidence suggests that it is no higher than that found among the ordinary child population of this age. There is, however, one marked difference. Contrary to the consistent finding of a greater proportion of boys than girls being emotionally disturbed, there is a higher incidence among our girls. Might this be because appearance is more important to them from an earlier age and hence a physical, visible handicap causes more acute unhappiness to a girl?

The emotional adjustment of the group as a whole is a high tribute to the loving care and acceptance which must have been given by the parents from the earliest years onwards. It could be that the public's sympathy and concern have been of help to them in coming to terms with their own, very natural, feelings of shock and anxiety. Possibly too, knowing the cause has eliminated or at least reduced one common source of unhappiness and even friction between the parents, i.e. the urge to find the reason for having a handicapped child which often leads to endless probing, searching, questioning, guilt, doubt and mutual recrimination. To be able to lay the blame at a drug's door makes the situation less intensely personal and more objective than suspecting the healthy history of either parent. All this is, however, merely speculative and might be well worth exploring in a future study.

No doubt it helped, too, that the children are, generally speaking, attractive to look at, emotionally responsive and of normal intelligence. At the same time, it is a great achievement to steer such a wise and balanced course between providing emotional security and setting high enough standards so as to promote this remarkably satisfactory development. But clearly complacency would be dangerous if it ignored the fact that the children are still very young and that adolescence will inevitably force them to face even more difficult emotional problems and decisions.

The number of completely rejected children is small. In each case the home background is very disturbed so that the child's handicap is more likely to have been a contributory rather than the main factor determining parental inability or refusal to care for him. That the type of severity of defect is not of primary significance is also suggested by the fact that of the four most severely maladjusted children, one has a minor and the other a moderate disability.

(e) Home background and parental attitudes

The socio-economic level of the families was roughly similar to that in the population at large, the majority being in social class III and IV, i.e. non-manual, skilled and semi-skilled manual. A few children came from vulnerable or socially deprived homes. Family size was also quite similar to the general pattern in the country. The proportion of only children was comparable too, suggesting that a deliberate decision to have no more children was no more common in our group of parents than in the population generally.

The hope that the child should eventually be capable of leading an independent life and earning his living was shared by all parents. Education was rightly seen to be of immense importance, especially for those who have little or no use of their hands. Ambitions tended to be high and the question whether a child would be capable of reaching the required academic standard was rarely raised.

The incidence of stressful circumstances was high: in a quarter of the families one or both parents showed symptoms of emotional strain or there were impaired relationships between the parents, or between them and the child. Our study can offer no evidence on the extent or the degree to which the child's disability contributed to the disturbed emotional climate of the home; that it was not the main causative factor is obvious from the facts as known.

The evidence suggests that the presence of a very severely disabled child in a family produces one of two diametrically opposed and extreme situations: either the parents cope admirably, indeed heroically, and the child thrives almost as well as any normal one; or the family proves unequal to the tremendous strain, the mother breaks down, the marriage founders and the child is either wholly rejected or causes tension and dissent which are inevitably reflected in his own maladjustment.

(f) Achievement and adjustment in relation to physical impairment and environmental circumstances

A composite score was worked out for each child to make possible some overall assessment both of his present development and of the difficulties confronting him. In some 40 per cent of cases development was found to be almost optimal and the handicapping conditions were near minimal; for the majority the disabilities were found to be severe or very severe, and so was their effect on the various developmental aspects.

Achievements and adjustment were explored in relation to environmental conditions, particularly parental attitudes. As expected, the children in the most favourable environment showed the most satisfactory all-round functioning, irrespective of the severity of their physical disability. When achievement and adjustment were examined in relation to the degree of physical disability, the same trend was found: the less severely handicapped showed the more satisfactory intellectual, educational and emotional functioning; however, this was irrespective of environmental circumstances.

Perhaps what emerges most strongly from these findings is the close and inextricable relationship between endowment on the one hand and environment on the other; and the futility of trying to predict or assess the effect of either endowment or environment in isolation. Thus two children whose disability is very similar, will function very differently in different environments; and identical environments may lead to very different development depending on the type and degree of handicap.

3. Present and future educational needs

(a) Summary of the present situation
The majority of the children are being educated in ordinary schools alongside normal children. About a third are attending special schools for physically handicapped or hearing-impaired pupils; all but 10 per cent are in day schools. In terms of tested intelligence, the children at fee-paying schools – be these private or local authority – are the brightest, and those in special schools dullest; while the pupils attending State primary schools are markedly more able than those in special schools of one kind or another.

This situation is largely due to the selection criteria which determine a child's schooling. Fee-paying schools require a minimum level of intellectual ability which automatically excludes the average and dull child. Admission to special schools is governed by a more complex set of circumstances. The simplest is availability – if a child would have to leave home in order to attend one, he is usually first given the chance of going to an ordinary day school. Next severity of disability and the need for special educational methods are taken into consideration. Then the child's ability to hold his own educationally and to fit into school life, socially and emotionally, plays a part in the decision whether or not special schooling is recommended. In consequence, children in ordinary primary schools tend to be less severely handicapped, more intelligent and emotionally better adjusted than those attending special schools.

Once in a special school, there are a number of factors which are likely to depress still further the child's level of educational attainment: a shorter school day; fatigue due to a lengthier journey to get to school; and probably most important of all, there is likely to be not only a lower standard of work (because there will be a high proportion of dull children) but probably also a lower level of expectation on the part of the teachers. For the majority of pupils this is entirely appropriate, all the more so as it becomes increasingly the practice to try to retain handicapped disabled children in ordinary schools wherever possible. But the corollary of such a policy is that the severely handicapped intelligent child may not always find himself sufficiently stimulated educationally and challenged intellectually in a special school unless small group as well as individualised teaching methods are adopted. Of course, this difficulty is in no way specific to thalidomide children but applies equally to all handicapped children of good intelligence who attend special schools.

On the other hand, special schools have been in the vanguard of individualisation, i.e. making the curriculum and teaching methods fit the individual child rather than the other way round. Not only is the number of children passing Certificate of Education examinations increasing, but some schools also arrange for their bright pupils to go part-time to neighbouring secondary schools to benefit from their specialist teachers or equipment. It must be borne in mind that the children in our study were only at the beginning of their educational careers. A slow and gentle start is appropriate and unlikely to prejudice eventual scholastic success. Indeed, the contrary may well be the case since early discouragement and failure is cumulative while early enjoyment of school and learning augur well for later progress.

(b) Present needs and problems

The key question of the whole study is whether or not this group of children is receiving the most suitable education to enable them to develop their assets to the fullest extent possible. Our evidence suggests that this may not be the case altogether. Two further questions then follow: what is the extent and cause of this under-functioning? Can and should anything be done about it by the present school or is a change of school indicated?

Using as a yardstick the present level of educational functioning, a sizeable proportion have limited achievements in the basic subjects.

According to their teacher's assessments, about one in three (30 per cent) are backward in reading and two in five (40 per cent) in arithmetic, while one in four (24 per cent) are backward in both subjects. When pupils in special schools are considered, their reported level of attainments is much lower overall than that of those in ordinary schools.

Of course, it can be argued that there is no cause for concern as there is a similar degree of backwardness among non-handicapped children of this age; furthermore, because the children are still young and at an early stage in their primary schooling, there is plenty of time for them 'to catch up'. Moreover, there are several factors which – singly or in combination – are likely to have a deleterious effect on educational attainment. To begin with, a teacher's natural compassion for a disabled pupil may make her lower her demands and expectations, possibly quite unintentionally and even subconsciously, especially in ordinary schools where he is likely to be the only handicapped child. Next, absences from school are inevitable – the more frequent the more disabled the child – for hospital attendance, surgery, limb-fitting and other treatments. Next, a greater degree of emotional stress is equally inevitable due to having to come to terms with being 'different'; if one accepts the close link between emotion and learning, then one would expect the task of adjusting emotionally to the handicap to be to some extent at the cost of educational progress – the more so in the light of the remarkably high degree of emotional adjustment achieved by this group of children.

Therefore one can justifiably argue that they are doing even better than one could have hoped for, in view of the multitude of problems with which they have to cope. This is undeniably the case. Suggesting that there might nevertheless be reasons for posing the question whether the backward children should not be helped to do better in no way detracts from their very creditable achievements so far. The reasons are twofold: first, educational success is emotionally satisfying and exciting for every child; being deprived of so many opportunities open to other children, especially in games and art work, educational progress is one avenue where the handicapped can equal or outshine his contemporaries; of course, all ought to be given educational help but as resources are scarce, perhaps the need of the physically handicapped is greater. Secondly, taking the long perspective, reaching the highest possible achievement matters more to the physically handicapped child just because he will depend more on his ability to use his intelligence than those who have the option later on of manual work at various degrees of skill – many of these are closed to the handicapped.

Even if educational levels could be raised, should it be done? It is difficult to give an unqualified 'yes', because it is known that undue educational pressure may be harmful and lead to emotional difficulties of various kinds. It would only be worth attempting provided that what is done in the way of enriched, remedial and more challenging teaching, is carefully tailored to the needs of the individual pupil; and provided his emotional adjustment is kept under close surveillance. Mere exhortation or worse still disapproval of present performance without positive, well-planned measures would do more harm than good. Similarly transferring a child to an ordinary school in the hope that the higher standards there will be an incentive and challenge, is to take an over-simplified and possibly destructive view. In the same way, it would be a mistaken sacrifice if parents made a special effort to find the necessary fees and had their child coached in the hope of gaining entry for him to a fee-paying school. At present it is difficult to see even the abler but very handicapped children fitting readily into their high-pressure environment. If there were to be a chance of satisfactory placements, considerable flexibility and adaptability to a child's problems and deficits would have to be introduced.

Indeed, two children at present in such schools are already finding it difficult to cope, despite quite reasonable intelligence. There are also two children in ordinary schools who would benefit from reduced educational standards and who might in fact do better in special schools.

How might higher educational functioning be achieved? By special individual tuition and assignments; by remedial teaching; by a heightened awareness among teachers concerning the positive value of adopting higher expectations; and, perhaps above all, by acceptance of the fact that challenging, enriching and stretching a child's mind is not synonymous with educational pressure or intensive coaching. Given appropriate help and given that at least a proportion of the children will be able to respond to it by accelerated progress, then it might be possible to recommend some children in special schools for transfer to ordinary schools. Each case would have to be given careful consideration to decide whether and when such transfer would best be made – for some pupils a delay until the secondary stage may well be advisable. Whether any transfer takes place or not, there is little doubt that higher educational achievement could become not only a source of emotional and intellectual satisfaction for a greater number of these handicapped children; but it would also be advantageous from the point of view of secondary schooling and later vocational choice.

Now to consider for how many children a change of school is indicated. At present, the great majority, three out of every four children, are receiving schooling suited to their age, ability and aptitude. Those likely to benefit from different educational provision fall into two groups of approximately the same size: for some eight children a more taxing, stimulating environment is likely to be more appropriate while the converse applies to a similar number, namely, they need either a less demanding or a more specialised curriculum. The former group are at present attending special schools and the latter are in ordinary or fee-paying primary schools. A summary of the changes suggested is shown in Table 17.

Table 17 Suggested changes of school

Present schooling	No change	Suggested change
Ordinary primary $N = 43$	37	3 – to school for physically handicapped or for educationally subnormal 1 – to school for the deaf 2 – to school for the partially hearing
Fee-paying primary $N = 8$	6	1 – to ordinary primary 1 – probably as above but too early to decide
Special school for the physically handicapped $N = 19$	11	3 – to ordinary school, provided there is a positive response to remedial teaching 4 – try 'stretching' and then consider later for transfer to ordinary school 1 – if hearing impairment confirmed, transfer to school for partially hearing
Special school for the deaf $N = 6$	5	1 – transfer to school for the educationally subnormal or, if none available, to a mental subnormality hospital
Special school for the partially hearing $N = 3$	3	No change

(c) *Likely future needs*

Educational forecasting is always a hazardous undertaking, the more so the younger or the more atypical the children; in both cases, unpredictable changes are not unlikely. Since this group of handicapped children contains such a wide range of disabilities, spans the normal range of intelligence and educational attainment, and is only just moving into the junior school, predictions about likely future educational needs can only be very tentative and provisional. A reassessment of progress made within the next two to three years is essential, if proper educational guidance is to be offered.

On present showing it looks as if some thirty children will be able to go on to ordinary secondary schools; that some twenty-eight will require special education of some kind or another; and that about twenty-two pupils would benefit from a grammar or technical secondary course. Eventually at least ten to fourteen children may be able to take advantage of tertiary education, be this at a university, a technical college or a college of education.

7. Conclusions and Recommendations

In intellectual ability, level of educational attainments and emotional adjustment, the children closely resemble the general child population of this age. The opportunity of having received preschool education appears to have had beneficial results and it would be desirable to extend similar facilities to all the handicapped. Although overall our group is physically severely damaged, more than half could well hold their own in ordinary day primary schools; only about a third required special schooling of one kind or another.

On the one hand the conclusion is justified that considering the many problems the children have to cope with, their scholastic performance is better than one might have expected. On the other hand there are grounds for arguing that being enabled to reach the highest possible educational achievement matters even more to the handicapped child just because he will depend more than normal children on his intellectual abilities in finding employment. Hence the extent of educational under-functioning which was found must cause concern. Whether steps should be taken to remedy it, is not an easy question to answer.

At present the emotional and social adjustment of the children is very satisfactory and again little different from that found among ordinary children. Educational pressure is known to be harmful and can lead to emotional difficulties of various kinds. Therefore any attempt to raise the level of educational functioning for a proportion of the children needs to be carefully considered and if decided upon, carried out with care and constant vigilance. Providing more challenging, enriched or remedial teaching would have to be suitably adapted to the needs of each individual pupil; this is different from intensive coaching, both in method and in expectation since quick and short-term results are neither sought for nor expected. Rather the emphasis needs to be on the therapeutic value of success, the fact that improved educational achievement can be a source of emotional and intellectual satisfaction.

Given such help, a number of children may then benefit from transfer to ordinary schools but this should be decided on the basis of their response to special programmes to accelerate their rate of learning. For a number of children the struggle to hold their own with normal children is proving too difficult and their transfer to special schools seems advisable.

Overall then, it looks as if about 20 per cent of the British thalidomide population will require very considerable special care; their educational needs will present serious and long-term problems and will almost always involve special schooling including residential facilities for some children.

What of the future? A tentative conclusion is that eventually over half the children will be able to proceed to ordinary secondary, grammar or technical schools and quite a number on to tertiary education of some kind. However, a strong case can be made for reexamining the whole group within the next three years or so, and then again a year or two before the children are due to leave school. First, because few if any have had a comprehensive, multiprofessional assessment which ought to be the basis for long-term educational and vocational planning. Second, because for many of the children, adolescence is bound to be accompanied by serious emotional and social problems; advice and guidance to the parents beforehand may prevent or at least ease some of these difficulties. Third, many of the parents have doubts and anxieties which could be ameliorated by making available to them a psychological counselling service. A re-examination of the children could provide an opportunity to explore in depth the kind of regular short-term and long-term help which would be most appropriate and welcomed by them. Fourth, a great deal could be learned from such a follow-up examination about the intellectual educational and emotional pattern of development since intensive and continuous studies of handicapped children are far too rare; if it were extended to cover disabled children with similar handicaps but not caused by thalidomide, valuable comparative data would become available. Not only is there a need for much more research in this field generally, but the dearth of long-term studies is particularly marked.

In this connection it was found that children affected by thalidomide cannot really be regarded as a homogeneous group; even the much publicised limb deficiencies are not a feature shared by all. On the other hand, an equally serious – and in some cases more serious – handicap which has hitherto been given little attention, is impaired hearing which affected at least a third of the children studied. Also many of them have more than one handicap. Though overall the physical impairment is severe, the degree of handicap covers a very wide range. In functional terms, the differences are even greater.

An equally wide range was found in respect to psychological aspects. Moreover, neither intellectually, emotionally nor educationally did the thalidomide damaged children present any features or problems which are unique to them. Therefore, the conclusions drawn from this study can be applied equally to physically handicapped children generally, and particularly to those with multiple disabilities.

In the long run the successful integration of the handicapped child into the life and work of his community depends on his emotional and social adjustment. Thus far the development of these children is a great tribute to the loving care and acceptance which their parents have given them, and to the skill and attention of various specialists and of teachers. It is to be hoped that this favourable development will continue. However, a review of past studies which have compared the handicapped with those who have no disabilities has shown the former to be less mature and more disturbed. At the same time, both the consensus of opinion and the weight of evidence seem fairly heavily balanced against the view that the physically handicapped are inevitably maladjusted (Pringle, 1964). There seems to be general agreement that parental attitudes towards the child and his handicap are of paramount importance. To quote some early American workers (Allen and Pearson, 1928): 'The child seems to adopt the same attitude to the disability that his parents do. If they worry about it, so does he. If they are ashamed of it, he will be sensitive too. If they regard it in an objective manner, he will accept it as a fact and will not allow it to interfere with his adjustment.' This view is summed up most succinctly by one who himself succeeded in triumphing over very severe physical disability: 'Success or failure does not depend on what we lack but rather upon the use we make of what we have' (Carlson, 1941). The evidence of this study only serves to underline this truth.

Recommendations

1. A more challenging, enriched educational environment should be provided for the educationally under-functioning child as well as more specific remedial teaching where appropriate. Such provision must be adapted to individual needs and great care must be taken to avoid it becoming a source of emotional stress.
2. A change of school should be considered in about a quarter of the cases. In some instances this will involve a transfer to a special school, in others the move would be from a special to an ordinary school.

3. Long-term plans – which, must of course, be kept under review – ought to be made for the children's secondary and tertiary education as well as for their vocational needs.
4. Adolescence is likely to bring new and probably quite serious emotional problems which should be anticipated now by setting up a psychological counselling service both for parents and for children.
5. All the children should be re-examined within the next three years and again at least a year before they leave school.
6. The principles underlying the above recommendations also apply to physically handicapped children generally; in addition, as preschool education appeared to have beneficial effects on later educational progress, there is a strong case for making it available to all young handicapped children.

Appendix A. List of tests and other assessment procedures

I. Intellectual and language development

1. Terman–Merrill Intelligence Scale (Form L–M) – verbal test.
2. English Picture Vocabulary Test, Brimer and Dunn.
3. Raven's Coloured Matrices, a non-verbal test.
4. Goodenough-Draw-a-Man, a non-verbal test.

II. Educational attainments

1. Burt–Vernon Reading Vocabulary Test.
2. Neale Analysis of Reading Ability (Form A), giving comprehension, speed and accuracy scores.
3. Mental Arithmetic Test (specially designed for the National Child Development Study, 1958 Cohort.)
4. Teacher's assessment of child's achievement level in reading and arithmetic, made on a four-point scale.
5. Specimen of handwriting.

III. Emotional and social adjustment

1. Bristol Social Adjustment Guides completed by teachers.
2. Porteus Mazes (all but the first ten cases seen).
3. Three wishes and ambition for future job.
4. Observations of behaviour during interview, testing and play periods, made by the examining psychologist.
5. Reports from parents.

Appendix B. Mean Intelligence Quotients

Tests	'Authentic' thalidomide $\mathcal{N} = 60$	Thalidomide excluding profoundly deaf $\mathcal{N} = 53$	Thalidomide profoundly deaf only[1] $\mathcal{N} = 7$	Doubtful thalidomide $\mathcal{N} = 9$	Non-thalidomide $\mathcal{N} = 11$
Terman–Merrill	97·4	101·5	66·0	102·5	111·4
English Picture Vocabulary	96·5	101·0	—	95·9	107·3
Raven's Matrices	93·5	96·8	—	98·5	106·0
Goodenough Draw-a-man	86·8	87·5	79·4	89·2	95·5

[1]Only two deaf children were able to respond to the English Picture Vocabulary and matrices tests; hence no results are quoted. Nor can the Terman–Merrill result be regarded as a reliable indicator of their ability; it is given to show that on directly comparable material these seven children are inevitably very retarded because of their communication difficulty.

Appendix C. Mean Intelligence Quotients According to Type of School

	Ordinary primary	Fee-paying	All ordinary	Physically handicapped	Total[1]
No. of children	40	8	48	19	67
Test					
Terman–Merrill	106·1	118·5	108·2	94·48	103·6
English Picture Vocabulary	103·5	113·8	105·4	95·42	102·3
Raven's Matrices	98·9	112·7	101·2	95·94	99·7
Goodenough Draw-a-man	91·47	103·25	93·44	77·47	88.9

[1]This excludes schools for the deaf and the partially hearing, which are attended by ten children.

Appendix D. Reading Levels on Two Tests According to Type of School

| | Ordinary primary $N = 40$ | | Physic. Handic. $N = 19$ | | Fee-paying $N = 8$ | |
	Burt/Vernon	Neale	Burt/Vernon	Neale	Burt/Vernon	Neale
Advanced	7 (18%)	16 (40%)	—	—	3	4
Average	16 (40%)	7 (18%)	1 (5%)	3 (16%)	2	1
Backward	9 (22%)	2 (4%)	8 (42%)	1 (5%)	1	—
No score	8 (20%)	15 (38%)	10 (53%)	15 (79%)	2	3

Appendix E. Composite Rating Scores

For physical impairment, intellectual functioning, educational achievement, emotional social adjustment and environmental circumstances. (The higher the score, the greater the handicap)—maximum score = 5 for each aspect.

Case No.	Physic. impairmt.[1]	Intell. funct.[2]	Educ. achiev.[3]	Emot./Soc. adjust.	Envir. circs.[4]	Total score
1	2	3	3	3	3	14
2	2	3	2	1	1	9
3	3	5	3	2	2	15
4	4	3	4	1	2	14
5	2	3	4	1	3	13
6	3	3	2	1	2	11
7	4	3	4	2	2	15
8	5	2	1	1	1	10
9	4	3	1	1	1	10
10	4	3	5	3	5	20
11	3	2	2	3	1	11
12	3	3	4	4	2	16
13	5	5	5	5	3	23
14	3	3	4	5	3	18
15	4	3	3	1	1	12
16	2	4	3	2	2	13
17	5	4	5	3	5	22
18	5	3	3	2	2	15
19	3	3	4	4	2	16
20	2	2	3	1	1	9
21	4	3	3	1	3	14
22	3	1	1	1	1	7
23	3	3	4	1	2	13
24	2	4	3	2	2	13
25	3	4	5	3	2	17
26	3	4	4	2	5	18
27	4	3	4	2	1	14
28	2	2	1	2	1	8
29	4	3	3/4	2	1	13
30	5	4	5	3	4	21
31	1	2	3	3	2	11
32	3	2	3	1	2	11
33	3	3	1	1	1	9
34	5	3	2	5	3	18

Case No.	Physic. impairmt.[1]	Intell. funct.[2]	Educ. achiev.[3]	Emot./Soc. adjust.	Envir. circs.[4]	Total score
35	2	1	1	1	1	6
36	3	3	5	2	3	17
37	2	3	3	3	1	12
38	4	3	3	1	2	13
39	1	2	3	1	1	8
40	5	3	2	5	3	18
41	5	5	5	5	5	25
43	1	2	2	1	1	7
44	1	2	3	2	1	9
45	2	4	3	2	2	13
46	2	3	3	1	2	11
47	3	2	3	1	1	10
48	1	4	3	3	3	14
49	1	2	3	1	2	10
50	4	3	4	2	4	17
51	3	3	4	5	3	18
52	1	3	3	3	3	13
53	1	2	2	4	2	11
54	5	3	5	2	1	16
55	2	2	1	1	1	7
56	5	5	5	5	4	24
57	3	3	3	4	2	15
58	3	4	5	5	3	20
59	1	1	1	1	1	5
60	2	4	4	5	4	19
61	1	3	1	2	1	8
62	1	1	2	1	1	6
63	1	3	2	1	2	9
64	1	3	3	4	2	13
65	1	3	3	1	1	9
66	1	3	3	2	2	11
67	1	3	3	2	1	10
69	5	3	5	3	5	21
70	2	1	1	2	3	9
71	4	3	3	3	2	15
73	5	3	2	1	1	12
74	1	2	2	1	1	7
75	3	4	4	4	4	19
76	3	3	2	4	2	14
77	3	5	5	5	2	20
78	1	3	3	2	2	11
79	3	3	3	1	1	11
80	3	3	2	1	1	10
81	3	3	2	1	1	10
82	5	3	2	1	2	13
83	2	2	1	1	1	7

[1]Minimal impairment = 1. Maximal = 5.

[2]Intellectual Rating: 130+ = 1, 115–129 = 2, 85–114 = 3, 70–84 = 4, 69 and below = 5. (This combines scores from 5 tests.)

[3]Very good educational achievement = 1. (This combines reading and arithmetic.)

[4]Very favourable environmental circumstances = 1.

Appendix F. 'Outcomes' in Relation to Environmental Circumstances

Most favourable environmental circumstances
= 1. $\mathcal{N} = 30$

Case no.[1]	Intell. funct.	Educ. achiev.	Emot./Soc. adjust.	Total score
2 (2)	3	2	1	6
8 (5)	2	1	1	4
9 (4)	3	1	1	5
11 (3)	2	2	3	7
15 (4)	3	3	1	7
20 (2)	2	3	1	6
22 (3)	1	1	1	3
27 (4)	3	4	2	9
28 (2)	2	1	2	5
29 (4)	3	3	2	8
33 (3)	3	1	1	5
35 (2)	1	1	1	3
37 (2)	3	3	3	9
39 (1)	2	3	1	6
43 (1)	2	2	1	5
44 (1)	2	3	2	7
47 (3)	2	3	1	6
54 (5)	3	5	2	10
55 (2)	2	1	1	4
59 (1)	1	1	1	3
61 (1)	3	1	2	6
62 (1)	1	2	1	4
65 (1)	3	3	1	7
67 (1)	3	3	2	8
73 (5)	3	2	1	6
74 (1)	2	2	1	5
79 (3)	3	3	1	7
80 (3)	3	2	1	6
81 (3)	3	2	1	6
83 (2)	2	1	1	4
	71	65	41	177
Mean score:	2·3	2·2	1·4	5·9

[1]Degree of physical impairment in brackets.

Favourable environmental circumstances = 2
$N = 27$

Case no.[1]	Intell. funct.	Educ. achiev.	Emot./Soc. adjust.	Total score
3 (3)	5	3	2	10
4 (4)	3	4	1	8
6 (3)	3	2	1	6
7 (4)	3	4	2	9
12 (3)	3	4	4	11
16 (2)	4	3	2	9
18 (5)	3	3	2	8
19 (3)	3	4	4	11
23 (3)	3	4	1	8
24 (2)	4	3	2	9
25 (3)	4	5	3	12
31 (1)	2	3	3	8
32 (3)	2	—	1	3
38 (4)	3	3	1	7
45 (2)	4	3	2	9
46 (2)	3	3	1	7
49 (1)	2	3	1	6
53 (1)	2	2	4	8
57 (3)	3	3	4	10
63 (1)	3	2	1	6
64 (1)	3	3	4	10
66 (1)	3	3	2	8
71 (4)	3	3	3	9
76 (3)	3	2	4	9
77 (3)	5	5	5	15
78 (1)	3	3	2	8
82 (5)	3	2	1	6
	85	82	63	230
Mean score:	3·2	3·0	2·3	8·5

[1]Degree of physical impairment in brackets.

Average environmental circumstances = 3
$\mathcal{N} = 13$

Case no.[1]	Intell. funct.	Educ. adjust.	Emot./social achiev.	Total score
34 (5)	3	2	5	10
36 (3)	3	5	2	10
40 (5)	3	2	5	10
48 (1)	4	3	3	10
51 (3)	3	4	5	12
52 (1)	3	—	—	3
58 (3)	4	5	5	14
70 (2)	1	1	2	4
1 (2)	3	3	3	9
5 (2)	3	4	1	8
13 (5)	5	5	5	15
14 (3)	3	4	5	12
21 (4)	3	3	1	7
	41	41	42	124
Mean score:	3·2	3·2	3·2	9·6

[1]Degree of physical impairment in brackets.

Unfavourable environmental circumstances = 4
$\mathcal{N} = 5$

Case no.[1]	Intell. funct.	Educ. achiev.	Emot./soc. adjust.	Total score
30 (5)	4	5	3	12
50 (4)	3	4	2	9
56 (5)	5	5	5	15
60 (2)	4	4	5	13
75 (3)	4	4	4	12
	20	22	19	61
Mean score:	4·0	4·4	3·8	12·2

[1]Degree of physical impairment in brackets.

Very unfavourable environmental circumstances = 5
$N = 5$

Case no.[1]	Intell. funct.	Educ. achiev.	Emot./soc. adjust.	Total score
10 (4)	3	5	3	11
17 (5)	4	5	3	12
26 (3)	4	4	2	10
41 (5)	5	5	5	15
69 (5)	3	5	3	11
	19	24	16	59
Mean score:	3·8	4·8	3·2	11·8

[1]Degree of physical impairment in brackets.

Appendix G. Outcomes in Relation to Degree of Physical Impairment

Minimal physical impairment = 1
$N = 18$

Case no.[1]	Intell. funct.	Educ. achiev.	Emot. adjust.	Total score
31 (2)	2	3	3	8
39 (1)	2	3	1	6
43 (1)	2	2	1	5
44 (1)	2	3	2	7
48 (3)	4	3	3	10
49 (2)	2	3	1	6
52 (3)	3	3	3	9
53 (2)	2	2	4	8
59 (1)	1	1	1	3
61 (1)	3	1	2	6
62 (1)	1	2	1	4
63 (2)	3	2	1	6
64 (2)	3	3	4	10
65 (1)	3	3	1	7
66 (2)	3	3	2	8
67 (1)	3	3	2	8
74 (1)	2	2	1	5
78 (2)	3	3	2	8
	44	45	35	124
Mean score:	2·4	2·5	1·9	6·8

[1]Rating of environmental circumstances in brackets.

Minor physical impairment = 2
$\mathcal{N} = 16$

Case no.[1]	Intell. funct.	Educ. achiev.	Emot. adjust.	Total score
1 (3)	3	3	3	9
2 (1)	3	2	1	6
5 (3)	3	4	1	8
16 (2)	4	3	2	9
20 (1)	2	3	1	6
24 (2)	5	3	2	10
28 (1)	2	1	2	5
33 (1)	3	1	1	5
35 (1)	1	1	1	3
37 (1)	3	3	3	9
45 (2)	4	3	2	9
46 (2)	3	3	1	7
55 (1)	2	1	1	4
60 (4)	4	4	5	13
70 (3)	1	1	2	4
83 (1)	2	1	1	4
	45	37	29	111
Mean score:	2·8	2·3	1·8	6·9

[1]Rating of environmental circumstances in brackets.

Moderate physical impairment = 3
$N = 22$

Case no.[1]	Intell. funct.	Educ. achiev.	Emot. adjust.	Total score
3 (2)	5	3	2	10
6 (2)	3	2	1	6
11 (1)	2	2	3	7
12 (2)	3	4	4	11
14 (3)	3	4	5	12
19 (2)	3	4	4	11
22 (1)	1	1	1	3
23 (2)	3	4	1	8
25 (2)	4	5	3	12
26 (5)	4	4	2	10
32 (2)	2	3	1	6
36 (3)	3	5	2	10
47 (1)	2	3	1	6
51 (3)	3	4	5	12
57 (2)	3	3	4	10
58 (3)	4	5	5	14
75 (4)	4	4	4	12
76 (2)	3	2	4	9
77 (2)	5	5	5	15
79 (1)	3	3	1	7
80 (1)	3	2	1	6
81 (1)	3	2	1	6
	69	73	60	202
Mean score:	3·1	3·3	2·7	9·1

[1]Rating of environmental circumstances in brackets.

Severe physical impairment = 4
$\mathcal{N} = 11$

Case no.[1]	Intell. funct.	Educ. achiev.	Emot. adjust.	Total score
4 (2)	3	4	1	8
7 (2)	3	4	2	9
9 (1)	3	1	1	5
10 (5)	3	5	3	11
15 (1)	3	4	1	8
21 (3)	3	3	1	7
27 (1)	3	4	2	9
29 (1)	3	4	2	9
38 (2)	3	3	1	7
50 (4)	3	4	2	9
71 (2)	3	3	3	9
	33	39	19	91
Mean score:	3·0	3·5	1·7	8·2

[1]Rating of environmental circumstances in brackets.

Maximal physical impairment = 5
$\mathcal{N} = 13$

Case no.[1]	Intell. funct.	Educ. achiev.	Emot. adjust.	Total score
8 (1)	2	1	1	4
13 (3)	5	5	5	15
17 (5)	4	5	3	12
18 (2)	3	3	2	8
30 (4)	4	5	3	12
34 (3)	3	2	5	10
40 (3)	3	2	5	10
41 (5)	5	5	5	15
54 (1)	3	5	2	10
56 (4)	5	5	5	15
69 (5)	3	5	3	11
73 (1)	3	2	1	6
82 (2)	3	2	1	6
	46	47	41	134
Mean score:	3·5	3·6	3·1	10·2

[1]Rating of environmental circumstances in brackets.

Appendix H.

Name	*Age*	*Nature of handicap*	*School*
Ellen	6 yr.	Bilateral upper limbs. Short arms (elbow length) three fingers each side; left handed; reach difficult; head down on page, turned to right always	Physically handicapped

		Retarded	Below average	Average	Above average	Able	Comments
Intellectual functioning	Verbal			X			
	Practical/non-verbal			X			Somewhat weak at spatial relationships
	Vocabulary			X			
	Reading			X			A little below average for age group but progressing satisfactorily at school
Educational achievements	Number			X			
	Writing/drawing manual control			X			Writing and figures neat. Has considerable manual dexterity but expressive work rather tiny and constricted
Emotional and social adjustment		Generally good but shows a few minor signs of unsettledness; rather timid and unforthcoming. Slightly immature and lacks independence at present					

Present and likely future educational needs

Ellen's disability is not handicapping her educationally, particularly as she has considerable dexterity. She is not quite working to her full capacity, possibly because diffidence prevents her seeking extra stimulation. A relatively undemanding environment may be helpful in view of her timidity but she may be capable of responding to somewhat greater expectations. Later on, Ellen might well manage in an ordinary school (as other equally impaired children already do), but the more sheltered conditions of a special school may continue to be more appropriate to her all-round needs. Eventual occupational choice may be somewhat limited but no serious difficulty need be anticipated.

Name	Age	Nature of handicap					School
Eileen	7 yr.	Bilateral upper limbs. No arms, not even 'flippers'. Uses *left* foot. Prefers feet to prosthesis					Ordinary primary

	Retarded	Below average	Average	Above average	Able	Comments
Intellectual functioning						
Verbal					X	Definitely verbally superior
Practical/non-verbal				X		Rather poorer at mazes. Average spatial perception
Educational achievements						
Vocabulary					X	Speech very good
Reading					X	Excellent reader; fluent, accurate and very good comprehension
Number				X		Meticulous in all her work
Writing/drawing manual control				X		Writing good but expressive work less firmly controlled
Emotional and social adjustment	Very stable and well adjusted. Socially mature and very balanced all round emotional development. A great credit to all concerned					

Present and likely future educational needs

Making excellent progress in normal school despite severe disability and can be expected to continue to advanced education. Her talents lie definitely on the verbal side and with intelligence and personality assets so much above the average, no serious difficulty need be anticipated in overcoming some inevitable limitation of occupational choice. Well able to profit from any mechanical aids which become available.

Name	Age	Nature of handicap						School
Helen	6 yr.	Bilateral lower limbs; nasal deformity; vision and hearing suspect. No legs except 2 inch long stalks at hip level from which feet protrude. Nasal speech (passage obstructed—three operations only partially successful)						Physically handicapped residential
		Retarded	Below average	Average	Above average	Able	Comments	
Intellectual functioning	Verbal			X			Verbal reasoning rather poor	
	Practical/non-verbal			X			Practical ability and intelligence as assessed by drawing about average	
Educational achievements	Vocabulary		X				Fluent but lacks understanding	
	Reading		X				Educational achievements very limited and behind her potential	
	Number		X					
	Writing/drawing manual control						Writing and figures reasonably good but lacks control in any free drawing. Average maturity level	
Emotional and social adjustment							Somewhat unsettled. Socially very eager for acceptance but simultaneously shows signs of unconcern and 'writing off' of adults. Not fully adjusted to variable environment between holidays at home and school terms in institution, but has considerable resilience	

Present and likely future educational needs

Schooling is appropriate in character but Helen is under-functioning in relation to her ability. Unless remedial teaching can enable her to catch up, particularly on the verbal side, she is unlikely ever to be able to manage in the normal stream. Psychosocial stresses may well be more handicapping than her physical disability. The contribution of a hearing defect to her current retardation requires investigation. Helen's occupational choice is likely to be restricted and she may require special practical training and sheltered conditions.

Name	Age				School
Peter	8 yr.				Ordinary primary

Nature of handicap

Unilateral lower limb. Right leg deformed and amputated at knee level at twelve weeks. Extra thumb on right hand amputated at six weeks—no manipulative difficulty at all now. Hearing suspect

		Retarded	Below average	Average	Above average	Able	Comments
Intellectual functioning	Verbal		X				The assessment of his verbal ability may be an under-estimate because of his impaired hearing
	Practical/non-verbal		X				
Educational achievements	Vocabulary		X				Deafness is likely to continue to interfere with his educational progress
	Reading		X				
	Number		X				
	Writing/drawing manual control						Fairly mature but lacks strength
Emotional and social adjustment		Though there are some minor signs of unsettledness, he is generally stable and well adjusted. Partial deafness puts him at disadvantage socially and may account for some diffidence and some inability to concentrate					

Present and likely future educational needs

Peter's physical defect does not handicap him unduly educationally and he should continue to manage in an ordinary school provided that sufficient allowance is made for his impaired hearing. If, however, remedial teaching does not enable him to keep up with his classmates, special education for this disability may be desirable in his own long-term interest.

Name	*Age*	*Nature of handicap*						*School*
Paul	6 yr.	Unilateral lower limb. Right leg deformed and amputated at knee level at ten weeks. Extra thumb on right hand amputated at six weeks – no manipulative difficulty at all now. Hearing suspect						Ordinary primary
			Retarded	Below average	Average	Above average	Able	Comments
Intellectual functioning		Verbal			X			Verbally rather better than on practical tests
		Practical/non-verbal			X			
Educational achievements		Vocabulary			X			As he had been taught by the I.T.A. method, assessment on a test employing traditional materials put him at a disadvantage for the time being. Average achievement reported by his school
		Reading			X			
		Number			X			
		Writing/drawing manual control			X			
Emotional and social adjustment		Stable and well adjusted. Almost over-confident and rather intolerant of failure. Developing normally. A credit to all concerned						

Present and likely future educational needs

Paul's defect is not a handicap educationally and he should continue to manage satisfactorily in an ordinary school. His achievements were still too limited to enable any reliable prediction to be made about future potential; no special difficulties need be anticipated.

Name	Age	Nature of handicap	School
Terence	6½ yr.	Bilateral upper limbs. Asthmatic. Speech indistinct. No arms except for one tiny digit at right shoulder. Works entirely with feet which he prefers to prosthesis	Physically handicapped

		Retarded	Below average	Average	Above average	Able	Comments
Intellectual functioning	Verbal			X			
	Practical/non-verbal						
	Vocabulary			X			Speech sometimes indistinct
	Reading		X				Somewhat retarded considering his level of intelligence though average for his age
Educational achievements	Number		X				Number concepts and memory good
	Writing/drawing manual control			X			Firm grip with feet and control good. Mature level
Emotional and social adjustment		Stable and well adjusted generally (though perhaps a little over anxious about adult approval). Lively, very resilient and very independent. Socially mature and a credit to all concerned					

Present and likely future educational needs

Terence's general development is good but educationally he is not attaining the standards which might be expected considering his level of general ability. His severe physical defect is a handicap, particularly in slowing down his output. Special school is undoubtedly the correct placement for him but he may well require more stimulation and encouragement to enable him to realise his full potential. Some remedial teaching or extra tuition should be considered if he continues to function at an average level during the next two years. His general ability and personality assets are such that he will probably continue to adjust satisfactorily at each stage and to profit from all the facilities made available to him.

Name	Age			School
Ronnie	6½ yr.			Ordinary primary

Nature of handicap

Unilateral lower limbs. Right foot protrudes at knee. Left foot also weak and requires support. Left eye squint. Ear trouble: possibly defective hearing; very poor articulation

	Retarded	Below average	Average	Above average	Able	Comments
Intellectual functioning						
Verbal		X				
Practical/non-verbal	X					
Educational achievements						
Vocabulary		X				Speech poor, requires therapy. Almost impossible to follow because of poor articulation
Reading		X				
Number		X				
Writing/drawing manual control			X			Control good

Emotional and social adjustment

Ronnie is showing signs of very serious maladjustment, with very varied symptoms including considerable hostility to others. He has some strength of personality and independence and may become much better able to cope in a less demanding and, to him, frustrating environment

Present and future likely educational needs

In view of both his physical handicap and his limited intellectual ability, Ronnie would be more appropriately placed in a special school where he could receive more individual attention and make progress at his own pace. His occupational choice is likely to be restricted and he may require special training and placement at that stage.

Name	Age				School
Martin	6¼ yr.				Ordinary primary

Nature of handicap

Bilateral upper and lower limbs. No legs. No arms other than four fingers each side just below shoulder level. Right side 'arm' longer than left with rudimentary elbow and inward twist of 'hand'

	Retarded	Below average	Average	Above average	Able	Comments
Intellectual functioning						
Verbal			X			
Practical/non-verbal			X			
Educational achievements						
Vocabulary		X				Under-achieving in relation to his capacity. May require remedial teaching.
Reading		X				
Number		X				
Writing/drawing manual control		X				Manual control neat. The level of his drawing was immature
Emotional and social adjustment						Somewhat unsettled. Confident and socially precocious to a certain degree but resistant and hostile in novel or frustrating situations. Considering the severity of his handicaps to which are added environmental difficulties, he is coping better than might be expected

Present and likely future educational needs

Martin's physical disabilities are so severe that special school education is quite essential. At present he is retarded in all aspects of learning and the need for remedial teaching at a later stage must be borne in mind. However, his need for a more taxing or more stimulating environment together with more academic pressure, has to be balanced against his need for security and for a stable environment. Since he is severely handicapped by multiple disadvantages. his learning difficulties may well be linked to the many stresses with which he is confronted.

Name	Age	Nature of handicap				School
James	7½ yr.	Bilateral upper limbs. Short arms with three fingers on both; inwardly twisted 'hands'. Holds pencil between outer two fingers				Ordinary school

		Retarded	Below average	Average	Above average	Able	Comments
Intellectual functioning	Verbal		X				Variable standards between tests but generally did rather better on the non-verbal side
	Practical/non-verbal		X				
Educational achievements	Vocabulary		X				Working at about his own level
	Reading		X				
	Number		X				Computation good
	Writing/drawing manual control			X			Neat, tidy, controlled work
Emotional and social adjustment		Moderately unsettled and emotionally immature for his age. Insecure and rather ill-at-ease, almost suspicious					

Present and likely future educational needs

James seems to be managing reasonably well in his school situation despite his handicap and his somewhat limited ability. With sufficient emotional support he may also be able to cope with ordinary secondary education but increasing demands may necessitate additional care and possibly more individual attention. Physical limitations make it likely that he will require special occupational training.

Name	Age		School
Len	6 yr		Ordinary primary

Nature of handicap

No limb defect. Ears deformed (low fleshy lobes only), and hearing impaired. Asthmatic; heart defect; possible visual defect and speech very indistinct

	Retarded	Below average	Average	Above average	Able	Comments
Intellectual functioning						Len's drawings suggest that he may have more ability than was evident on any of the formal tests. Moreover, the results of these and of subsequent tests of educational achievement may all be unreliable because of his impaired hearing; he has made little or no scholastic progress and will inevitably fall further and further behind his age group. His basic level was barely that of a four-year-old
Verbal	X					
Practical/non-verbal	X					
Educational achievements						
Vocabulary	X					
Reading	X					
Number	X					
Writing/drawing manual control		X				
Emotional and social adjustment						

Very disturbed, unsettled behaviour and a great many signs of maladjustment. Very 'babyish' for his age and treated as such

Present and likely future educational needs

It seems clear that Len is unable to manage in an ordinary school and that he will inevitably become increasingly retarded unless he is given special educational treatment for his hearing disability. Ideally, special education in a school for the deaf is required, but in the absence of local provision, and in view of his probably limited intellectual endowment, he might derive more benefit from the specialist facilities and more individual attention available in a class for the educationally subnormal provided his hearing defect is taken into account.

References

ALLEN, F. H. and PEARSON, G. H. J. (1928) 'The emotional problems of the physically handicapped child'. *British Journal of Medical Psychology*, **8,** 212–35.

BUROS, O. K. (1965) *The Sixth Mental Measurements Yearbook*. New Jersey, Gryphon Press.

CARLSON, E. R. (1941) *Born that way*. New York, John Day.

CARNEGIE UNITED KINGDOM TRUST (1964) *Handicapped Children and their Families*, Dunfermline.

KERSHAW, J. D. (1961). *Handicapped Children*. Heinemann Medical Books.

MALLINSON, V. (1956) *None can be called deformed*. Heinemann.

PRINGLE, M. L. KELLMER (1964) *The Emotional and Social Adjustment of Physically Handicapped Children*. Occ. Publ. No. 10, N.F.E.R., Slough, Bucks.

PRINGLE, M. L. KELLMER (1965) *Deprivation and Education*. Longmans.

PRINGLE, M. L. KELLMER, BUTLER, N. R. and DAVIE, R. (1966) *11,000 Seven-year-Olds*. Longmans.

TIZARD, J. and GRAD, J. C. (1961) *The Mentally Handicapped and their Families*. Oxford University Press.

WRIGHT, B. A. (1960) *Physical disability: a psychological approach*. New York, Harper.

Subject Index

PB–04076
5–22